FF 00 00

00 FF 00

00 00 FF

www.color

ROGER PRING

SERIES CONSULTANT
ALASTAIR CAMPBELL

WATSON-GUPTILL
PUBLICATIONS
New York

To Sarah, Sally and Katy

First published in the United States in 2000 by Watson-Guptill Publications, a division of BPI Communications, Inc., 770 Broadway, New York, NY 10003

A catalog record for this book is available from the Library of Congress.

ISBN 0-8230-5857-3

This book was conceived, designed, and produced by The Ilex Press Limited
The Barn, College Farm
1 West End, Whittlesford
Cambridge CB2 4LX
England

Sales Office:
The Old Candlemakers
West Street, Lewes
East Sussex BN7 2NZ
England

Editorial Director:
Sophie Collins
Art Director:
Alastair Campbell
Managing Editor:
Shuet-Kei Cheung
Editor:
Peter Leek
Additional material:
Howard Oakley
Web research:
Graham Davis
Designers:
Graham Davis and Roger Pring
Illustrations:
John Woodcock, Alastair Campbell, Julian Baker

Originated and printed by Hong Kong Graphic, Hong Kong

INTRODUCTION

Color is painless and very nearly automatic. On screen, you can use any color you like, including many that you never see in nature. You can create landscapes of cinematic complexity and splendor; sweeping gradients of brilliant hues, jewel-studded and intersected by glowing shafts of light; cornucopias of intensely desirable images displayed against infinite vistas of total chromatic perfection. You can see them, even now, in your mind's eye, detailed and gleaming. Can your vision be shared?

Color on the Web is complex and needs careful management. On screen, you are likely to be limited to an apparently arbitrary palette that includes colors you may wish never to see again. Your theater of action is limited to a little window whose size and quality is not yours to control, and within which anarchy may arise without notice. So, your glistening canvas must be taken down from the studio wall, sliced into tiny fragments, rolled up tightly and inserted into a thin and capricious tube for delivery to its audience. Despite all this, your vision can be shared; the colorfully seductive brilliance and saturation of the screen will conspire to make it memorable. Green for go.

Roger Pring

London

8

SEEING RED

R ed doesn't exist; neither does PANTONE® 485, nor flame-cherry vermilion gloss. The only real red is FF0000. Try this simple test to prove it—take a strawberry, a color-sample book, a lipstick, and a color monitor showing full-value red; put them in a room from which all light has been excluded, and observe.

The only red you see is on the screen. Electrons from the gun at the back of the tube bombard the screen phosphors and selectively excite the red ones. They glow, and you see red. Close your eyes, and pretty soon the equivalent shape in blue will appear on the inside of your eyelids. If you're later asked to describe the red you saw, you can recall its intensity but you can't describe the experience by reference to any other kind of redness. This red is unique to the screen—more intense than fruit, more memorable than a sample chip of color, and more seductive than lipstick.

The blue after-image signals that the inside of your eyes has been affected, though only temporarily, by this experience of red. Moreover, you may have undergone a subtle change of mood in a subliminal reaction to this chromatic exposure. An increased heart rate and a heightened predisposition to aggression or lust may ensue—so be careful when observing the test block (*above right*).

1 Concentrate hard on the black disk (*top*) for 15 seconds, then stare at the lower disk for another 15. One of the sensitive chemicals (rhodopsin) in the cones of your retinas will become temporarily bleached by exposure to red, and will interpret the white paper as a bright turquoise.

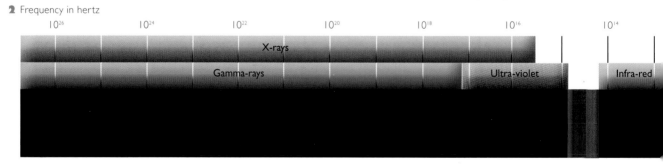

2 Frequency in hertz

10^{26}	10^{24}	10^{22}	10^{20}	10^{18}	10^{16}	10^{14}

X-rays

Gamma-rays
Ultra-violet
Infra-red

10

What is light made of?

Isaac Newton (1642–1727) used a glass prism to demonstrate that "white light" was actually composed of a range of spectral colors.

Through a tiny hole, he let a beam of sunlight into a completely dark chamber. Striking the prism, the light separated out fanwise into its constituent colors—from red at one end to violet at the other. Using a second prism, he was able to recombine the colored rays into white light. His assistant, possessing better color vision than his master, was able to discern seven colors: red, orange, yellow, green, blue, indigo, and violet.

Having seen how colors could be refracted, Newton went on to explain the means by which objects appeared "colored" using his theory of "corpuscles." He believed that all objects were covered with a microscopically thin layer of

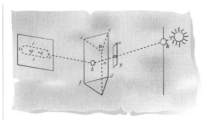

refracting cells, whose differing sizes determined an object's apparent color when irradiated with a continuous stream of light.

A hundred years later, Thomas Young discovered that light is not a stream of particles, but is made of a succession of waves. It is the size of these waves that determines their color.

At the end of the 19th century, James Clerk Maxwell went on to show that visible light forms only a small section of the electromagnetic spectrum. Colors could now be precisely described in terms of their wavelength.

3

Carrots, not surprisingly, contain a heavy dose of carotenoids. These pigments enthusiastically absorb shorter-wavelength (blue) light and reflect the longer(red/orange/yellow) frequencies.

3

11

10^{10}		10^{8}		10^{6}	

Radio waves

Microwaves

2

The electromagnetic spectrum (*left*) runs from radio waves that are several hundred meters long to very short (high-frequency) X-rays and gamma rays. Visible rays are in a tiny range, from 400 nanometers (blue) to 700nm (red).

AN EXPOSED PIECE OF THE BRAIN

In the competitive waters of the primordial swamp, organisms appeared whose brains had evolved to the point where external "buds" formed outside the brain case.

This apparently grisly development was the first stage in the formation of the human eye, and also accounts for the curious fact that the light-sensitive layers of the eye appear to be "inside out" from an engineering point of view. Light has to penetrate a layer of cells, which reduce its intensity before it strikes the vital receptors. This is also the cause of the receptor-less "blind spot" where the optic nerve has to make its necessary exit from the orb of the eye on its way to the brain.

The ancient wisdom of Euclid (c. 300 BC) was that the eye itself sprayed the passing scene with a stream of mysterious light, and colored objects achieved a temporary existence. The reality is exactly opposite, as we now smugly know. The red part of this strawberry has absorbed all other colors of the visible spectrum and radiates back only strawberry red. Even these r are not colored in the ordinary sense: they are just waves vibrating at the frequency of red light.

Finally, the eye focuses these waves on the retina, and the "red" rays excite tiny receptors especial sensitive to that wavelength. Near receptors react to "blue" and "gree rays, so the yellow seeds on the strawberry's surface activate the gree receptors also (yellow in these terms is red plus green), while the leaf is "seen" by the green receptor only. The resulting electrical activity sends signals along the opti nerve to the brain. Along this pathway the image is turned "right side up," and arrives in the lower part o the left hemisphere of the brain—which is where colc finally arises. About 30 percent of all the gray matter i the brain is concerned with image processing, while unknown millions of neural links deal with the tricky matter of choosing a "nice" color.

12

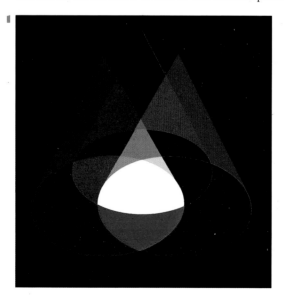

1 | 2

2

The additive system (*left*) is the basis of color management on screen. The three converging red, blue, and green lights produce white where they overlap; the only surprising result is the yellow made by red and green. The mixtures in the subtractive system (*right*) seem intuitively more familiar. These three colors plus a reinforcing black are the stuff of conventional paper printing.

Magenta

Yellow

How does the brain see?

Sitting at a computer screen, you might imagine the eye/brain combination to resemble a rather elaborate flat-bed scanner. The scanner, having recorded the image in successive passes, presents it to the computer as a stream of data that can be displayed on the screen, processed, and stored on a hard disk. Each bit of data has exactly the same status as its companions, and its electrical pulse is interpreted uniformly as part of the whole picture.

This analogy is entirely wrong. The part of the brain that handles visual stimuli operates on many more levels. The diagram shows the location of the processing areas. Some of their functions are understood; and some are effectively color-blind, dealing only with movement or dark/light boundaries. One section of the

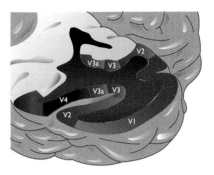

The back of the brain (*left*), with the "vision" areas of the left hemisphere. V1 deals with broad areas of depth and motion; the superior temporal sulcus processes motion only. V2, V3 and V3a are for edges, depth, and defined areas of color; V4 handles color only.

brain deals exclusively with color, and there is a smaller section that responds to color when defined by shape.

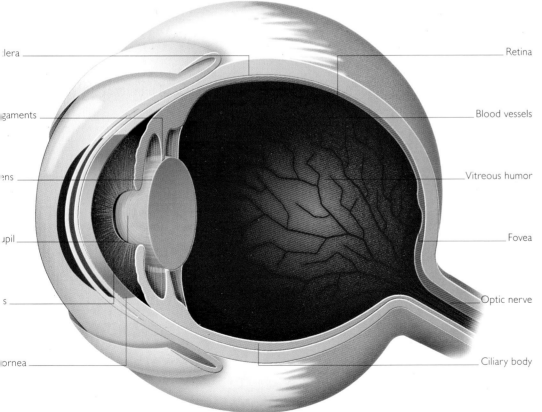

Sclera

Ligaments

Lens

Pupil

Iris

Cornea

Retina

Blood vessels

Vitreous humor

Fovea

Optic nerve

Ciliary body

3
The human eye (*left*) is an extraordinarily complex structure. At the front it has an elegant windshield equipped with a wiping system fed by a continuous stream of cleaning fluid; the center has a pressurized clear jelly that helps maintain the shape of the orb; at the back is a chemical film of electrically connected sensors that connect to the brain via a fine cable. In addition there is auto-focus, auto-exposure, and low-light capability. But no zoom, so far.

KEEPING IT REAL

K was for black. C was for cyan, M for magenta, and Y for yellow. So far so obvious (though K in fact stood for "key plate," since B could equally well have signified black or blue). These colors formed the pillars of print, and the inadvertent inclusion of RGB elements in a print job was as popular as coughing at a concert.

Now, in the purely electronic environment of the Internet, the old four-color set is equally unwelcome. In fact, the screen image routinely attains a higher range of color, contrast, and saturation than any kind of paper-based process. Naturally, there is a crossover where print-based designs need to be remanufactured for the screen, but there is no such constraining legacy for new design.

So, what could be better? A palette of brilliant saturated color with the ability to represent a wide contrast range, instant feedback and correction on screen, animation, sound, a global audience absolutely at home with the televisual image—surely, all is for the best in this best of all possible worlds? The gap in this apparently seamless scenario is the pinhead-sized blot on the landscape called bandwidth. Using a simple wired network the desktop computer can transmit hundreds of megabytes of data in very short order. The creaking telephone lines that now form the last link in the Internet delivery chain are very slow by comparison, easily overwhelmed by peaks in demand and choking over relatively tiny file sizes. Though a picture may paint a thousand words, in this environment words are more economical. To be precise, a thousand e-mail words would occupy 8k and an average 300-pixel-square RGB screen reproduction the Mona Lisa uses up 264k.

Time to go home. The old rosettes of the conventional four-color process (*left*). The enlarged section is magnified 1,300%. Compare these dots with the opposite.

14

2 | 3 | 4
A transparency
with a wide contrast
range—shown first
in four-color print (2),
then as a JPEG
on an 8-bit screen
(256 colors) (3),
and finally on a 24-bit
monitor (millions of
colors) (4).

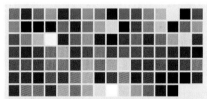

5
Reducing the same
image (*far left*) to
indexed color shows
the effect of dithering.
The choice of "exact
palette" during the
indexing process
results in a palette of
110 colors (*above*),
enough to preserve
the overall appear-
ance. The magnified
version shows the
pixel structure for
comparison only
(there is no magnifi-
cation on the Net).

MONITORING PROGRESS

In a conventional CRT (cathode-ray tube) monitor the screen image is made of glowing phosphors—organic chemicals that degrade progressively over time. A precisely repeating pattern (the "trio") of red, green, and blue dots is applied to the inside face of the screen, with a matching mask slightly to the rear. The electron guns at the rear of the tube activate each phosphor dot selectively as they sweep across the screen. There are two principal mask types: aperture grille and shadow mask (*see right*). This technology is at a mature stage of development, with a range of flat, or nearly flat, screens on offer. Extraordinary efforts, both optical and electronic, have produced monitors that occupy half the desk space of their ancestors—but the battle appears to be lost; the CRT is under attack from devices that dispense with its bulky glass tube and fearsome voltages.

The demand for laptops forced the pace of development of the current crop of LCD (liquid-crystal display) monitors. The properties of these crystals have been known for many years, but there is a great technical gulf between the familiar LCD calculator display panel and the multilayered structure of a color monitor. In these screens, colors are produced by selectively activating each of the minuscule transistors at the rearmost level of the back-lit screen. Each transistor is equivalent to a pixel, capped with a red, green, or blue filter, and the light output of the pixel is controlled by varying the voltage applied to the polarized panels that form the upper layers of the screen. A medium-size LCD monitor might contain a total of over two million RGB pixels. In spite of the extreme rigor of the production process, many screens contain a tiny proportion of faulty pixels that are either "dead" or permanently "lit." One screen manufacturer opines that 20 of these inactive pixels (0.0008 percent) per screen constitutes an acceptable fault level. If possible, check your screen before buying. Dead pixels can never be resurrected.

Further developments are afoot with FED (field emission display), otherwise known as PDP (plasma display panels). Currently these are employed for large-scale display, but monitor-size versions will arrive before long. The design is an elegant synthesis of CRT and LCD principles, but the reliance on phosphors currently means that such displays have a limited life.

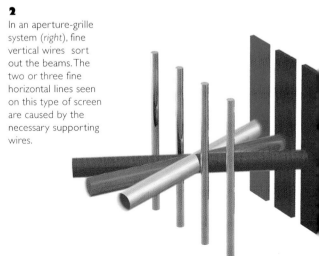

1
The shadow-mask grille (*right*) is shown much magnified. The mask's purpose is to ensure that the beam is accurately directed onto the relevant phosphor.

2
In an aperture-grille system (*right*), fine vertical wires sort out the beams. The two or three fine horizontal lines seen on this type of screen are caused by the necessary supporting wires.

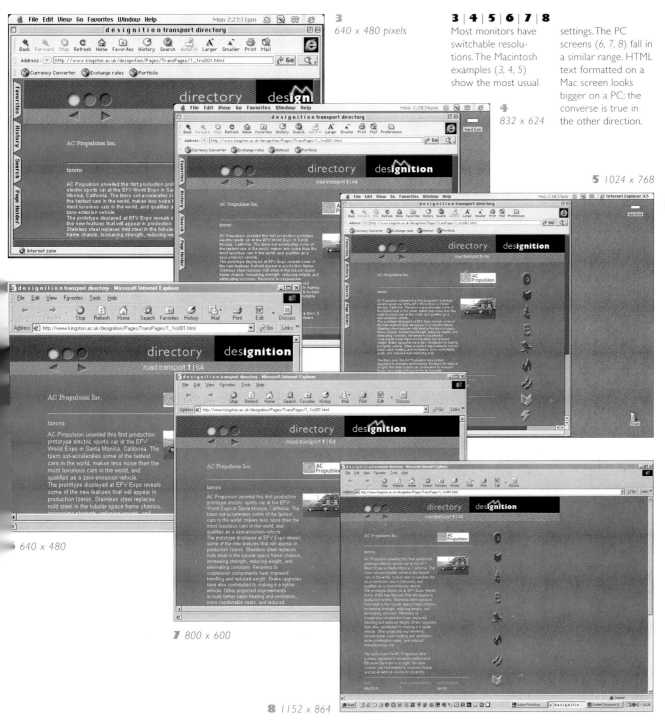

3
640 x 480 pixels

4
832 x 624

5 *1024 x 768*

6 *640 x 480*

7 *800 x 600*

8 *1152 x 864*

3|4|5|6|7|8
Most monitors have switchable resolutions. The Macintosh examples (3, 4, 5) show the most usual settings. The PC screens (6, 7, 8) fall in a similar range. HTML text formatted on a Mac screen looks bigger on a PC; the converse is true in the other direction.

LOST IN SPACE

There have been numerous attempts to formalize the description of color, resulting in a variety of competing standards. This is an area with a long history, and even longer shelves in technical libraries. The literature is concerned with dyestuffs, paint pigments, and printing inks, and the aim has been to create a standard that enables colors to be named, defined in mathematical terms, and reproduced accurately time after time.

When color arrived on computer monitors, there was no pressing need to define a standard for controlling the relationship between the screen image and the printed output. In those prehistoric times there was a meager spectrum containing eight colors—including black and white—and primitive printers struggled to output the results in shades of gray.

Fast forward through the last two decades of the 20th century to the present day. Nowadays even an average screen can show "millions of colors" while printers routinely interpret that screen image in "photographically real" terms. The demand for repeatability across a range

of devices is irresistible, driven by graphic-arts users who expect fidelity between their screens and the printed image. This is a hard row to hoe—between the multiplicity of software interests, the myriad technologies for delivering ink to paper, and the end user's capacity to administer a workable regime. Everyone has admirable intentions, but it's difficult to navigate through the marketplace to the holy grail of a solid system that will not cause more trouble than it cures.

The Web designer, though, may affect scorn toward this turmoil. After all, how can you go wrong with only 216 colors, many of which appear to be the same? If you design Web pages solely for your own offline consumption and never include elements that will have a printed existence elsewhere, possess a monitor that never wanders from a true color standard, never contemplate the possibility that the viewer might like to print your screen images in color, and believe that we shall be forever shackled by the "Web-safe" cube, then scorn away. The rest of us need to pay attention.

1 | 2 | 3 | 4

In the l*a*b color space, the full-color image (1) is expressed as three sets of values (or channels). The first in the sequence (2) has values for image brightness; the second (3) for values on the green/red scale; and the third (4) those for blue/yellow. In actual practice, only the first, light/dark, channel is useful for image manipulation. The other two are too counterintuitive for anything other than accidental effects.

The beginnings of color standardization

The Commission Internationale d'Eclairage (CIE) *defined a color system in the early 1930s that enclosed all the colors a normal human eye could perceive. The CIE "l*a*b" space* (right) *is familiar in the Photoshop color environment* (below), *though Photoshop dispenses with the asterisks. L denotes the color value on a light/dark scale; "a" its position along the green/red axis; and "b" its position along the blue/yellow axis. Unlike the RGB and CMYK spaces, l*a*b does not depend on measurements particular to any input or output device. This "device independence" makes it the preferred basis for producing*

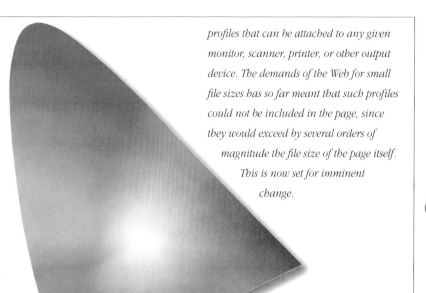

profiles that can be attached to any given monitor, scanner, printer, or other output device. The demands of the Web for small file sizes has so far meant that such profiles could not be included in the page, since they would exceed by several orders of magnitude the file size of the page itself. This is now set for imminent change.

19

2

3

4

BIT BY BIT

The period at the end of this sentence is about 0.3mm tall, slightly larger than one pixel on a typical color monitor. Though it may appear rather humble, such a pinprick is the end product of a considerable computing process. On a conventional CRT screen it is composed in its turn of three smaller phosphor dots, whose levels of red, green, and blue determine its overall value. This tiny trio, mingling with its neighbors, gives the illusion of color. If each of the three dots can be controlled to produce any one of 256 levels of intensity, you have "millions of colors" (actually, over 16 million [2^{24}] colors). In this 24-bit paradise, most colors of the visible spectrum can be shown or closely approximated. In the gloomier reaches of the real world, display inadequacies and lack of transmission bandwidth restrict the available palette to an 8-bit limbo; in this environment each pixel can produce only 256 different colors, though those 256 colors can be selected from a much wider palette (or color look-up table/CLUT).

1 | 2 | 3 | 4
The ubiquitous chameleon suffers in the cause of art. The 1-bit or "bitmap" image (*1*) is familiar from the candlelit era of screen imagery, while the 4-bit (16 colors) image (*2*) recalls slightly more recent machinery. 8-bit (*3*) delivers 256 colors and is the usual default for legions of domestic monitors. With 24 bits available (*4*) a full range of colors can be shown.

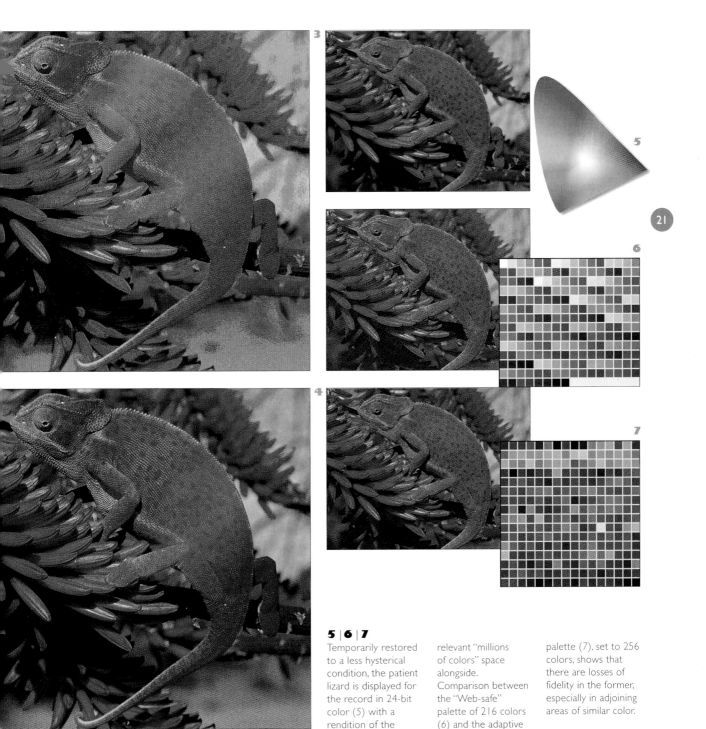

5 | 6 | 7

Temporarily restored to a less hysterical condition, the patient lizard is displayed for the record in 24-bit color (5) with a rendition of the relevant "millions of colors" space alongside. Comparison between the "Web-safe" palette of 216 colors (6) and the adaptive palette (7), set to 256 colors, shows that there are losses of fidelity in the former, especially in adjoining areas of similar color.

IN THE BLACK

Total color blindness is highly unusual. However, color confusion is widespread. It seems that about 10 percent of the male population suffers to some degree from protanopia (red-green confusion), though it is uncommon in women. It may also entail confusion between red and gray. Less common is the inability to distinguish between green and orange, or confusion between blue and green, or green and blue-gray.

These misapprehensions are physiological in origin. Much more interesting are the preconceptions that the eye—or rather, the brain—applies to the surrounding world. Studies by Edwin Land, inventor of the Polaroid instant-photo system, show that the brain has a great

capacity to interpret, or even to fabricate, color where none exists. In his experiments, a still life containing variety of differently colored and shaped objects was photographed with positive black-and-white film only first through a yellow filter and subsequently through orange one. The resulting transparencies, utterly devo of color, were then projected onto a screen through the same filters. As long as the pictures remained side by side, the audience could clearly see a strongly yel monochromatic image alongside a largely similar orar version. With the projectors repositioned to superimp the images exactly, almost all the colors of the origina scene were suddenly recreated.

The implication is inescapable: though the eye ma be a camera, the brain is more than just a roll of film. It responds to the difference in wavelengths and patte of light between the two images, and makes educated guesses at the colors of familiar objects. At a lower le the brain will see an apparently white surface as whit even though it may be illuminated with a very yellow tungsten lamp. This perceived "white point" is crucial all calibration procedures.

The "whiteness" of the blank lit screen is formaliz in three standards. After all, it would be fruitless to struggle to calibrate an image that was to be viewed alternately on a screen in a sunlit room, a fluorescent bright office, and a dimly lit garret. The principal standards are: D50 (warm yellow light at 5,000°K (degrees Kelvin)); D65 (6,500°K, which is equivalent midday sunlight); and 9300 (9,300°K for cooler daylig However, these are paradigms of perfection, since you are unlikely to have control over the eventual viewing conditions of the image.

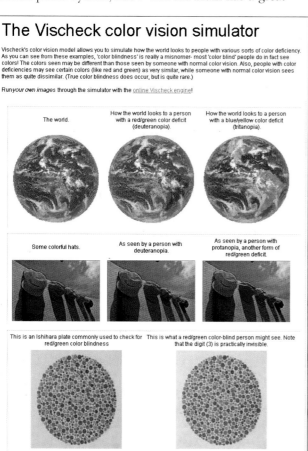

The Vischeck color vision simulator

Vischeck's color vision model allows you to simulate how the world looks to people with various sorts of color deficiency. As you can see from these examples, 'color blindness' is really a misnomer- most 'color blind' people do in fact see colors! The colors seen may be different than those seen by someone with normal color vision. Also, people with color deficiencies may see certain colors (like red and green) as very similar, while someone with normal color vision sees them as quite dissimilar. (True color blindness does occur, but is quite rare.)

Run your own images through the simulator with the online Vischeck engine!

The world.

How the world looks to a person with a red/green color deficit (deuteranopia).

How the world looks to a person with a blue/yellow color deficit (tritanopia).

Some colorful hats.

As seen by a person with deuteranopia.

As seen by a person with protanopia, another form of red/green deficit.

This is an Ishihara plate commonly used to check for red/green color blindness

This is what a red/green color-blind person might see. Note that the digit (3) is practically invisible.

www.vischeck.com (left) is where you can take a very informal test of your color vision.

Proper color testing is more demanding, and needs to be done by a qualified optometrist.

These screen images (*left*) give an approximation of the color cast differences between D50 (*1*), D65 (*2*), and 9300 (*3*).

The gamma question

There is a large obstacle to cross-platform screen harmony between Macs and PCs. Gamma is the measure of contrast displayed by a monitor, and traditionally it has been set at 1.8 for Apple Macintosh systems and 2.2 for PCs. The former has become the convention for print-based work, and the latter for the production of screen images. The example below shows uncorrected transfer between the two systems. Where gamma relates to color space, the higher (PC) value has the inherent property of showing more shadow detail in any given image. It is therefore important that images processed in one gamma environment be converted correctly whenever they are transferred to another.

Mac → PC

Mac ← PC

FINGER ON THE BUTTON

The routines outlined here are for the diligent. The hardware can be complex and some of the procedures tedious in the extreme, but the reward is a strikingly beautiful profile. The unifying purpose is to harmonize color input and output across all devices. Grounded in the early work of the CIE, it gathers all the characteristics of a given machine into one portable file.

The International Consortium on Color (ICC), founded in 1993, is a group of interested parties that administers ColorSync (for the Apple system) and the ICM standard (for Windows). Visit their Web site at **www.color.org** for a taste of the complexities behind the façade. The system depends also on the cooperation of device manufacturers in making available ready-made profiles to match each of their products.

This is an essentially reductive process. Anyone who has struggled with malfunctioning computer systems has already gained the costly wisdom that juggling variables in parallel is a recipe for premature aging and hair loss. What's required is a rock face with immovable pitons,

interlinked by taut ropes and leading to a brightly and truly colored summit. Profiles are the trusty handholds in this ascent; and if the device manufacturer can't or won't provide them, you must make your own. There are several competing software solutions (the procedures shown opposite are based on the ColorBlind Matchbox system). For the ultimate in accuracy, the essentials are a spectrophotometer and a certain amount of obsessive behavior. If you have less time, adequate color vision, and a smaller wallet, a good approximation can be obtained just by looking.

There is an evangelical aspect to these endeavors. In the age of man's chromatic innocence there was no need for color matching, and therefore no disagreement. As more devices come to the market, more contradictory voices are raised, more bizarre color-delivery systems compete for attention, and false prophets may be heard in the land. The ICC, however, appears to have staked out the moral high ground; let us hope that, under their guidance, all our screens will one day shine equally with the true light.

ColorSync/ICM and sRGB

There is a struggle in prospect between the ICC profiles system and the sRGB color space promoted by Microsoft and Hewlett-Packard. Whereas ColorSync/ICM attempts to deal with the whole supply chain from scanner and camera, through the "creative" software package, to eventual screen or print output, sRGB is at present concerned solely with the relationship between the software and the receiving monitor. The sRGB specification, if adopted by all manufacturers, would mean common qualities across all displays (the standard inevitably is based on Windows norms). It deals only with the average qualities of each device.

The most immediate effect of sRGB is for users of Photoshop, where the recent releases have sRGB as the default color space. Files created in color spaces other than sRGB (almost all for the immediate future) will open with a request for a conversion decision. Choosing "convert" may lead to a gross change in the overall color balance. Opinions differ as to the safest course of action; in the absence of an accurate printed confirmation of the original colors, it may be prudent to refuse conversion and employ intuition instead. Alternatively, change the default color space to one with which you are more confident.

Getting the color right

*On an adjustable monitor there are several routes to fine-tuning the screen image. Even the most basic display, with no apparent external controls, should be capable of adjustment by the system software. The user will see a sequence of test targets and can adjust the image for contrast and color balance. Part of the typical Macintosh calibration sequence is shown (*below left*).*

With the PANTONE Personal Calibrator, this operation is taken one stage further, using a thin plastic matrix applied to the screen surface. With this system, exact allowance can be made for the lighting conditions around the monitor. The end product is an ICC-compatible profile.

The basic ColorBlind Matchbox

system employs a detector with rubber suction feet. While attached to the screen, it computes the actual output of the RGB guns. It also allows for the ambient lighting conditions and produces an ICC profile.

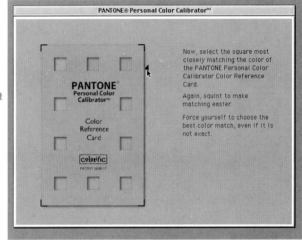

1

The Macintosh Monitor Calibration Assistant (*above*) leads the user through a set of fairly intuitive tests. This screen is the hardest of the five-screen sequence, requiring considerable squinting, blurring of vision, and twisting in the chair to establish the point at which the ubiquitous logotype merges most completely with its background. The built-in monitor profiles cover a wide range of devices.

2 | 3

The PANTONE Personal Calibrator displays a series of colored squares, produced by each of the RGB guns. You set the color balance by judging the point at which the relevant color seems about to fade. Finally, you apply the blue-plastic matrix (2) to the screen, adjust the lighting to normal working conditions, and attempt to match the perceived screen color to the actual color of the matrix.

4 | 5 | 6

The ColorBlind Matchbox system uses a miniature spectrophotometer (*below, far left*), which is applied to the screen (*left*). A read-out of the signal from each of the guns is displayed graphically (*below left*) and can be corrected on screen.

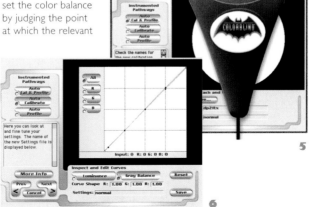

THE FURTHER PURSUIT OF PERFECTION

Delivery of accurate screen color is only part of the picture. Your ideal viewer may want to print out your page as a record, a souvenir, of a joyful chromatic experience. Others may simply want a quick (and possibly dirty) black-and-white print for information only. In the latter case, your artfully contrived rainbow background and meaningfully colored hierarchy of type is likely to dissolve into a morass of gray and similar dots. Sidestep this potential porridge by trying it for yourself as your page becomes more complex, or take a screen grab and check it out in a desaturated version.

The ideal viewer may use a less-than-ideal color inkjet printer, with a life-expired ink cartridge printing on highly unsuitable paper. There is no known cure for this disorder. Your page should be prepared, however, with the virtuous assumption that all this will one day change for the better. Spectrophotometer calibration systems like the one shown here are currently very costly; they are designed to close the loop between the screen and a variety of input and output devices. Fortunately some of their functions can be approximated by trial and error.

1 | 2
A dedicated color picker, like the one supplied by PANTONE (1), can be used within an image-editing or Web-page creation application to standardize Web-safe color between screen and print. The accompanying swatch book (2) also gives the color breakdown in RGB, CMYK, HTML, and Hexachrome.

3
The traditional print-based PANTONE system also appears in the form of a color picker (3) and swatch book. By definition, this is not a Web-safe environment—but for those working with the luxury of a 24-bit corporate intranet, for example, the business of matching corporate colors is made very straightforward.

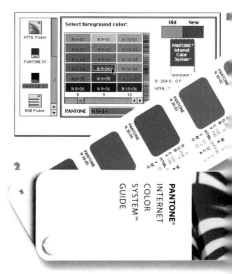

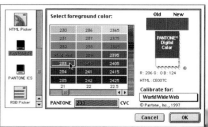

4
Sophisticated devices like the MatchBox ColorBlind spectrophotometer show how things could be in the best of all possible worlds. Having calibrated the monitor with the companion screen photometer (see page 25), a test print can be made from one of a series of built-in color test charts. In this case, a middle-of-the-road color inkjet printer is being calibrated. The resulting print is then measured square by square, following a series of prompts from the software. This rather tedious process is worth it for the true perfectionist—the result is a profile that precisely reflects the qualities of the actual device being used. Regular recalibration will take care of any changes in ink color or density. The test print can also be scanned or photographed, or output to film to provide profiles for a range of input and output devices.

5

On the Web itself there are many sites offering help with calibration. At the sophisticated end of the spectrum, DisplayMate offers a commercial service for the video, film, and TV industries. At (**www.displaymate .com**), Windows users can download a series of free charts like the one below. The Turkish Photography Circle (*right*) helps out, too, with monochrome and color charts, and a challenging text workout for your eyeballs.

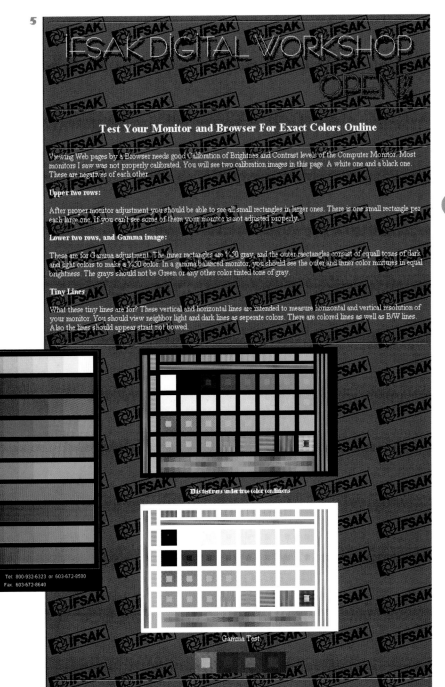

5

IFSAK DIGITAL WORKSHOP
OPEN!

Test Your Monitor and Browser For Exact Colors Online

Viewing Web pages by a Browser needs good Calibration of Brightnes and Contrast levels of the Computer Monitor. Most monitors I saw was not properly calibrated. You will see two calibration images in this page. A white one and a black one. These are negatives of each other.

Upper two rows:

After proper monitor adjustment you should be able to see all small rectangles in larger ones. There is one small rectangle per each large one. If you can't see some of them your monitor is not adjusted properly.

Lower two rows, and Gamma image:

These are for Gamma adjustment. The inner rectangles are %50 gray, and the outer rectangles consist of equall tones of dark and light colors to make a %50 color. In a gamma balanced monitor, you should see the outer and inner color mixtures in equal brightness. The grays should not be Green or any other color tinted tone of gray.

Tiny Lines

What these tiny lines are for? These vertical and horizontal lines are intended to measure horizontal and vertical resolution of your monitor. You should view neighbor light and dark lines as seperate colors. There are colored lines as well as B/W lines. Also the lines should appear strait not bowed.

This test runs under true color conditions

Gamma Test

Tune your monitor untill you can see all the recatngles in upper rows. Proper calibration means you miss no details in the dark and bright edges when viewing web graphics...

Email: info@displaymate.com
Web: www.displaymate.com

DisplayMate Technologies Corp
Color Scales Test Pattern
©1999 by DisplayMate® Technologies Corp.

Tel: 800-932-6323 or 603-672-8500
Fax. 603-672-8640

COLOR SCHEMING

Would you drive a purple car? While wearing a lime-green shirt? Would you let someone else tell you what constitutes a good combination of colors? Or let your computer decide it for you? There are complex influences at work in the matter of color choice. Some of these factors seem to be physiological, but most must be acquired through exposure to a particular outside world. The average citizen may have sensitivities allied to the color of the national flag. The average Inuit has allegedly more than two dozen words to describe the different colors of snow. The average Web-page designer has 216 colors to describe the appearance of everything in the known universe.

Leaving the difficult matter of taste aside for a moment, there is the additional constraint of the established conventions of link colors. Clickable links have been blue (0000FF) since year zero in the history of the Net, visited links purple (990099), and active links red (FF0000). These color settings are easily changeable, but at the risk of confusing the viewer.

In the interests of humanity, 140 colors of the Web palette have been blessed with names—and can be defined in more recent browsers by using those names rather than hexadecimal numbers. Earlier browsers will respond only to a select ten from this named list. None of the above gives any clue as to a strategy for choosing colors, though Web-authoring software packages sometimes kindly group colors by related hue values. Here we are in a purple car, wearing a lime-green shirt and wondering what looks nice. Enough prevarication. Nothing is to be lost by trial and error—the Web page, unlike the domestic interior, has an infinite capacity for absorbing ill-judged decisions. Take a published site that has a good color sense and analyze the HTML colors. Go a step farther and borrow that color scheme; then change the color values one by one.

Soon it will be obvious which are the pivotal colors

at the heart of the scheme. And also that it is color contrast, rather than the nature of the colors themselv that's at the root of successful color selection. Prove i making a screen grab of a good site and inverting the colors in an image-editing program. The chances are that, though it may appear strange, it still hangs toget

Try returning to the familiar artist's color wheel for from-the-ground-up view of how color choice works; visit Hot Door (at www.hotdoor.com) for a trial of their Harmony software (*see opposite*). Above all, remember that the viewer's eyeballs are temporarily in your care.

There are hundreds of models that attempt to describe the structure of color. This version of the familiar HSB (hue, saturation, and brightness) setup offers one of the more comprehe explanations.

a Hue

b Saturation

c Brightness (Lightness)

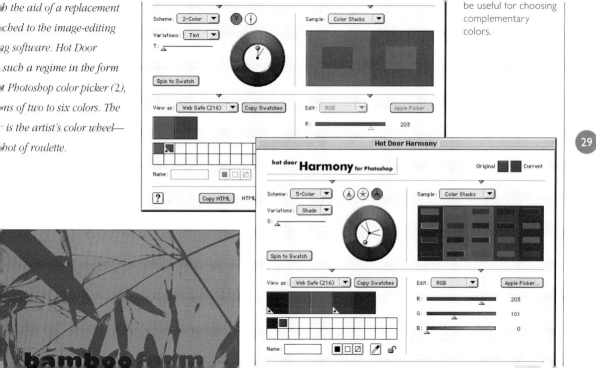

b the aid of a replacement
ched to the image-editing
g software. Hot Door
such a regime in the form
Photoshop color picker (2),
ns of two to six colors. The
is the artist's color wheel—
bot of roulette.

be useful for choosing
complementary
colors.

Scheme: 2-Color

Variations: Tint

T:

Spin to Swatch

Sample: Color Stacks

View as: Web Safe (216)   Copy Swatches

Name:

?   Copy HTML   HTML

Edit: RGB

R: 203

Apple Picker...

Hot Door Harmony

hot door **Harmony** for Photoshop

Original   Current

Scheme: 5-Color

Variations: Shade

S:

Spin to Swatch

Sample: Color Stacks

View as: Web Safe (216)   Copy Swatches

Name:

Edit: RGB

Apple Picker...

R: 203
G: 101
B: 0

bamboo

CHINESE WHISPERS

After the control of paper publishing, designing over the Web by Chinese Whispers (whereby information is passed through multiple sequential sources before it reaches you) is daunting. The whisper starts in Adobe Photoshop, perhaps, passing through exotic plug-ins before it reaches the Web page. When served back to the reader, it transits through a browser of indeterminate age and pedigree on anything from a high-end graphics workstation to a palm-sized portable.

The choice is to opt for either "safe color" or full color. Constrained to a "safe" palette of just 216 colors chosen by arithmetic rather than esthetics, graphics should pass fairly faithfully to the eye of the beholder. Images with continuous tones can only truly be safe if you are sure that the beholder will have more than 256 colors (8-bit color depth); such full color still requires careful preparation to ensure acceptably brief download times (lengthy waits are immensely frustrating).

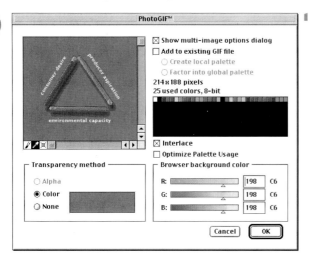

1

Your starting point may be the same as for printed work, but to get the best out of your pictures you need some additional tools and skills. Boxtop PhotoGIF (a Photoshop plug-in) gives fine control over the color and format of GIF files— including the use of transparency—and provides interlacing. This slices the image, TV style, into two sets of horizontal lines. The arrival of the first set can reassure the viewer that the download is in progress, the second fills in the missing areas to sharpen up the image.

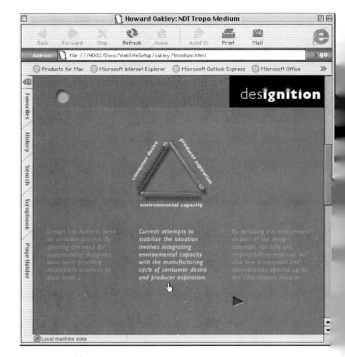

2

You have no control over the browser or platform on which a user will render your pages. Transparency could work well, as shown here in a recent version of Internet Explorer, but older browsers may not cope with it. You need to decide what risks you can afford to take, and then design and test accordingly.

3

HTML has scant support for color. It simply links the contents of a page together, leaving the recipient to render embedded graphics. Mark-up commands can color text, backgrounds, and borders, but even there you should take care to keep to cross-platform standards.

3

```
<html>

<head>
 <meta http-equiv="content-type" content="text/html;charset=iso-8859-1">
 <meta name="generator" content="GoLive CyberStudio 3">
 <title>Howard Oakley: NDT Tropo Medium</title>
</head>

<body bgcolor="#ccffff">
 <!--Version 4.0, 5 Apr 99, EHNO with GoLive CyberStudio-->
  
 <h1><font face="Times New Roman,Georgia,Times">NDT: The troposphere as a medium for propagation</fon
 <p><font face="Times New Roman,Georgia,Times">
 <hr>
 </font></p>
 <p><font face="Times New Roman,Georgia,Times">The troposphere is the lowest shell of our atmosphere,
 <ul>
  <li type="disc"><font face="Times New Roman,Georgia,Times">the lower troposphere, which extends up
  <li type="disc"><font face="Times New Roman,Georgia,Times">the middle and upper troposphere, from 3
 </ul>
 <p><font face="Times New Roman,Georgia,Times">Information about the troposphere comes from radiosond
 <p><font face="Times New Roman,Georgia,Times"><i>Folding of the tropopause, seen on the Aberystwyth
 <p><img height="331" width="363" src="tropfold.gif"></p>
 <p><font face="Times New Roman,Georgia,Times"><br clear="left">
 Prior to 1200, the tropopause appears to have been quite high, over 11 km above ground. At about 120
 <p><font face="Times New Roman,Georgia,Times">The substantial changes in radio refractive index in t
 <p><font face="Times New Roman,Georgia,Times">Crain, C M (1955) Survey of airborne microwave refract
 <p><font face="Times New Roman,Georgia,Times">Above the tropopause, changes in temperature and water
```

33

4

Previewed using just 256 colors, this page appears quite readable in Netscape Navigator on a Mac.

5

Moving up to "millions of colors" the colors in the graphic have desaturated but remain quite acceptable. However, the purple used to identify links has become too bright, making the text unreadable—something not seen in the authoring software. Check everything offline before going live, so problems can be traced through the sequence of stages and corrected.

SAFETY FIRST

Careful planning and a degree of experimentation are necessary for the execution of a "safe" color regime. In the right hands, graphic design work constrained to the 216 colors of the safe palette can look perfectly natural and remain every bit as good as unconstrained work.

Do not be afraid to employ dithering, either to enrich solid areas of color with the illusion of a third dimension or to extend the perceived range of colors beyond the 216. While dithering can detract from photographic images (particularly if performed on the viewer's computer), its skillful use in digital drawings can be very effective.

Dithering can also help you through strict color rules that clients may impose on logos and their ilk. At the outset, you should establish clear ground rules as to how you will achieve compliance, and then take great care to match colors.

1 | 2 | 3 | 4 | 5
The process of reducing the color palette of an image— as in the 216 Web "safe" palette— produces an effect of flat, hard-edged color bands (1). To compensate for the reduced palette you can use the technique of "dithering" in which the image pixels are redistributed in a predetermined pattern to create the illusion of a smooth transition from one color to another. Dithered patterns can be styled "diffusion," a random pattern which can be applied in variable amounts (2, with 50% dithering and 3, with 100%), "pattern"—a regular matrix of pixels (4), or "noise"—randomly placed pixels which decrease image definition (5).

6

6 | 7
Make sure that all the graphics and Web design applications that you use can display the Web-safe color palette. Although most are supplied with this as standard, you may need to make your own if using utilities like, for example, GraphicConverter. When creating new graphics, you can then restrict your work to safe colors. BoxTop's ColorSafe (7) is another Photoshop plug-in for safe dithered colors. If you need colors beyond the 216 available, mix from that palette to generate the desired effect. DitherBox (6) is a Photoshop plug-in that makes this process very easy by converting any RGB color into its nearest safe dithered equivalent.

7

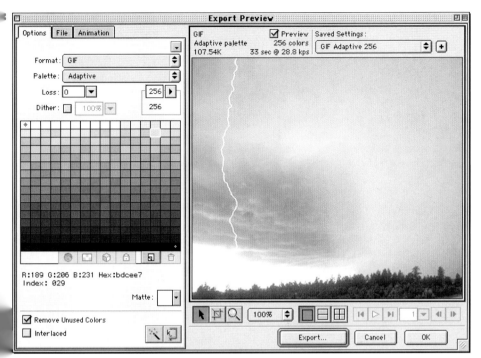

8
Fireworks' Export Preview is a powerful tool for previewing the effects of palette changes and dithering on images. This photograph has been rendered using an adaptive palette of 256 colors. Because its continuous tones cover a limited range of colors, it still looks very smooth and true to the original. Although not Web-safe, some adaptive palettes stand less chance of being significantly misrendered on client systems.

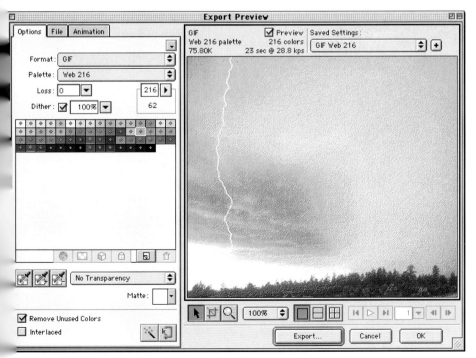

9
Dithered into safe colors, the sky breaks up into a mess of patches, some with obvious diagonal banding. In most cases, this type of image is best kept in deeper color (e.g., 32-bit JPEG), risking poor rendering only if the viewer's system can offer a mere 256 colors.

LOSS PREVENTION

Whether you're working with the continuous tones of photographic images (or digital painting), or drawings from desktop design software, Photoshop is a reliable and capable starting point for color work. Armed with the right plug-ins and techniques, its vast capabilities can almost always help you to find a way through problems.

When working with pictures, you should store them using a non-lossy format, such as Photoshop native files, and only apply lossy compression methods like JPEG as the final step before placing the pictures in Web pages. Repeatedly saving a file with JPEG

compression – which discards information at each 'save' – results in progressively deteriorating image quality.

Safe color images should be converted to indexed color (rather than RGB color) at an early stage, so that they remain within the safe palette. Moreover, because GIF compression doesn't discard any data, you can safely keep working files using that format.

Because mainstream Web graphics can't accommodate Postscript's fonts, curves, and color handling, Photoshop's built-in Postscript engine is also an invaluable tool for rendering EPS files created using Postscript design tools such as Adobe Illustrator and Macromedia Freehand.

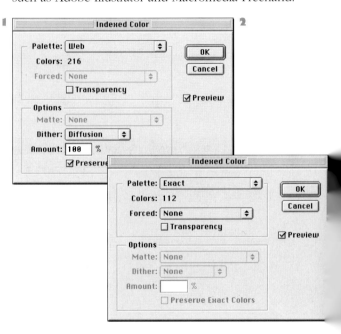

1
To create and save a safe color GIF in Photoshop, start with an RGB color picture.

2 | 3
Convert it into indexed color, using the 216 color "safe" palette for the Web (2). Diffusion dithering usually works best, although you may need to

experiment if the result is marred by dithering artifacts such as banding. Once in indexed color, switch back to RGB color and then return to indexed color (3).

You should now see an exact number of colors (equal to, or less than, 216) in the custom palette.

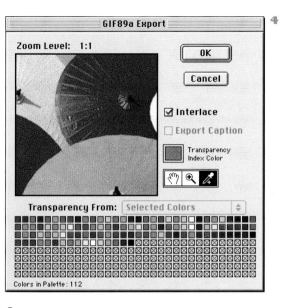

4

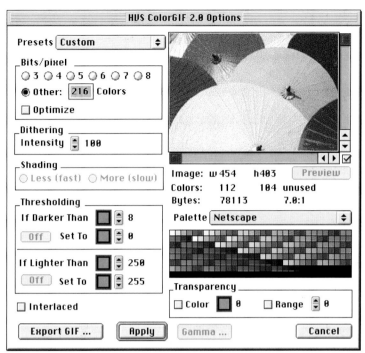

5

4

Finally, export the image in GIF89a format. You will then be able to set transparency and interlacing. The latter allows the viewer to see a blurred image during downloading, gradually becoming clearer as the whole file arrives.

5

Popular plug-ins that can make this easier still include HVS ColorGIF and BoxTop PhotoGIF. Although their interfaces are slightly different, each gives direct control over color depth and palette, and has GIF features such as interlacing and transparency.

6

If you have to use lots of smaller images—such as banners—on your pages, every few kilobytes saved makes a significant difference to the time it takes for the whole page to load. It is then worth spending time with a plug-in such as Boxtop ImageVice, whose purpose is to reduce the number of colors and the size of your image file.

LABOR SAVING

The legacy of nearly two decades of on-screen page make-up activity is a vast amount of that most precious commodity—content. The traditions of print mean there is an equally large amount of redundancy locked up in this material. From the Web perspective, there are billions of words with an excess of typographic styling and similar numbers of images of unnecessarily high resolution. A combination of three routes is the key to unlocking the potential of these pages. At a simple level, "old" pages can be turned into EPS files and re-manufactured into Web-ready GIFs. This crude approach mostly results in disaster, with reduced definition

mangling the words, though images can survive this treatment reasonably intact. Farther up the scale of effort, text content can be remade into HTML and the accompanying images brought out of CMYK into RGB at lower resolution. The most sophisticated solution is now provided by later versions of the original page make-up applications. This software offers an interface which comfortingly mimics the print-based techniques, while producing Web-ready output rather than files for film. Similar changes have taken place among the vector-based drawing applications. They now include anim-ation and powerful image optimization capabilities.

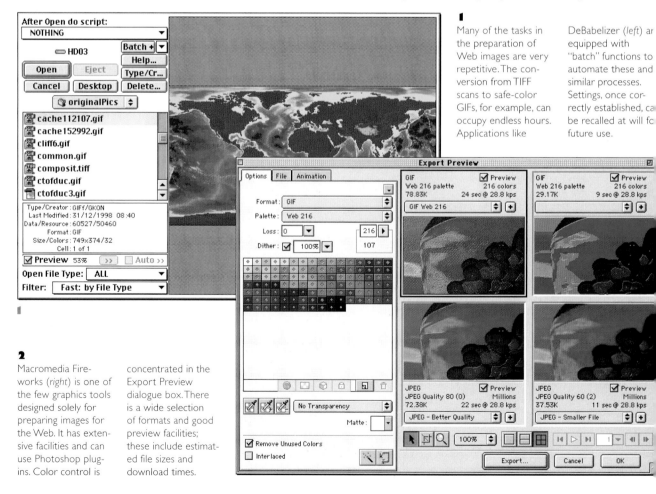

1

Many of the tasks in the preparation of Web images are very repetitive. The conversion from TIFF scans to safe-color GIFs, for example, can occupy endless hours. Applications like

DeBabelizer (*left*) are equipped with "batch" functions to automate these and similar processes. Settings, once correctly established, can be recalled at will for future use.

2

Macromedia Fire-works (*right*) is one of the few graphics tools designed solely for preparing images for the Web. It has exten-sive facilities and can use Photoshop plug-ins. Color control is

concentrated in the Export Preview dialogue box. There is a wide selection of formats and good preview facilities; these include estimat-ed file sizes and download times.

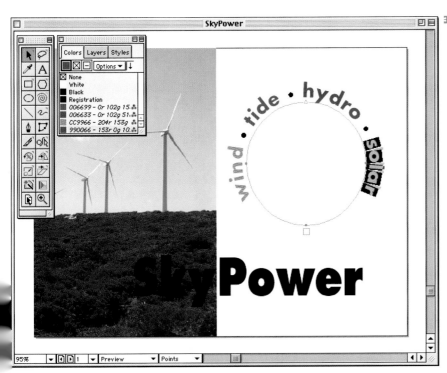

39

3 | 4

Early versions of
Freehand and its rival,
Illustrator, were used
for vector-based
drawing. These and
other applications
have now moved into
the territory of the
painting programs.
Type effects in Free-
hand (*left*) can now
be combined with
bitmap manipulation.
Note the color
palette (*far left*) with
safe colors loaded
from a built-in library.
The result can be
previewed (*above*)
within the application.

5 | 6

ImageReady is now
included in the
Photoshop package.
Pages developed in
the main application
can be optimized for
screen display in the
companion software
(*left*). The page is
sliced into sections
(*below left*), so that
various compression
settings can be tried.
The main image is
being tested at pro-
gressively coarser
JPEG settings. The
remaining graphic has
been saved as a small
GIF file, while the
background areas
make even smaller
files, saved as single-
color "no image"
slices.

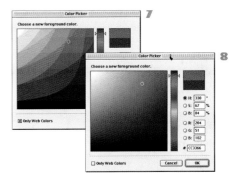

7 | 8

The banding in the
ImageReady color
picker (*above*) dem-
onstrates the limi-
tations of the Web-
safe palette when
compared with the
full-color version.

PAINTING BY NUMBERS

Although HTML is hardly color-centered, it does support limited use of color in text, backgrounds, and borders. Used judiciously, such color can be both aesthetically pleasing and safe across browsers and platforms. The same rule applies as for GIF pictures: confine colors to those in the palette of 216. However, in their effort to boast yet more features, major Web-authoring software packages offer a profusion of color palettes, as if to drag you away from safe color.

1
Dreamweaver offers standard HTML color schemes as style sheets. While these are guaranteed Web-safe, there are many more combinations—which can be equally effective and may appear less hackneyed. Each of the colors within these schemes is safe, not just the combinations offered.

40

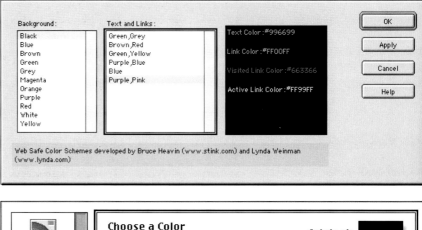

2
If you decide to use an authoring software package that doesn't offer such built-in facilities, or prefer to work with your own raw HTML, there are still tools to aid the safe use of color. SafePicker shows you numeric color values and helps you to paste them into HTML documents.

3
This color picker is constrained to Web-safe colors, working in RGB color space and in slider increments of 33 (hexadecimal).

4 | 5 | 6

Don't be tempted to use browser-specific named colors. Very few of them migrate successfully. Instead, keep to colors that are defined numerically, which cannot be misinterpreted by the HTML rendering engine in a browser. For instance, #FFFFFF is pure white and #000000 is black. In the example at right, the nearest color to "Cornflower blue" (4) is "#6699FF" (5). When offered by the package, HTML parsing and checking (6) should help spot any errors in your code—though you will probably need to check that your colors are Web-safe.

PHOTO QUALITY

The overwhelming majority of Web graphics are in JPEG or GIF format, despite the aspirations of the newer PNG specification and other contenders. As no single format yet meets the "one size fits all" requirement to supplant JPEG and GIF, this is likely to change slowly.

JPEG, often condensed into the MS-DOS extension .jpg was designed to store continuous-tone color images, like photographs and painted artwork, in space-efficient form. Because, to save space, its compression method simplifies the image content, it should serve as the final output format, and not be used for intermediate storage when you are working on images. The severity of compression is variable, with smaller file sizes resulting in poorer quality images; you should therefore, if your software permits, preview the effect of different degrees of compression before making a final commitment.

JPEG will effectively anti-alias sharp edges in the image and is thus rarely suitable for line art or digital drawings. In these cases, GIF is normally preferred, as it retains sharp edges and will not of itself cause anti-aliasing. Indeed, softening JPEG images with a gentle blurring filter can help them compress better.

JPEG retains full color information at 24-bit depth ("millions of colors") and has no facility for reducing the number of colors. However, it can contain information about image resolution, so you should ensure that the final output resolution is set to 72 dots per inch (dpi).

Progressive JPEG is a variant that works similarly to interlaced GIF in that the image is previewed during download, in blurry form; as it is not supported by Netscape browsers earlier than version 2.0 or Internet Explorer prior to 3.0, its use could result in a missing image on some systems.

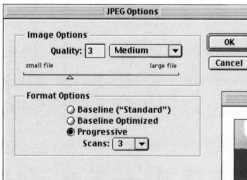

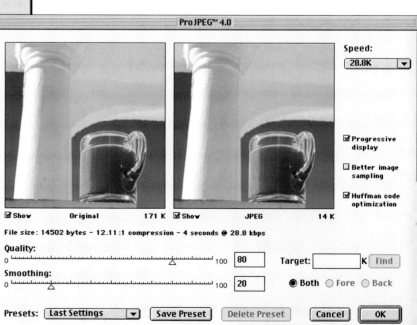

1
Photoshop's standard options for saving JPEG images are clean and simple, but they lack Fireworks's visual controls. Deciding the optimum compression in JPEG is of necessity an iterative visual process.

2
BoxTop's ProJPEG plug-in remedies that shortcoming well and allows you to build a library of presets for different types of pictures.

42

3 | 4 | 5 | 6

JPEG is a file format that uses a "lossy" compression method, meaning that some image data—and thus quality—may be lost during compression. The advantage of the JPEG format is that it can be used to display images in millions of colors rather than in the limited palette of GIF (which uses "lossless" compression techniques) and other formats. The degree of compression can be defined by you, but the more you apply, the poorer the quality of the displayed image. The examples show an image with varying amounts of compression, along with the original, uncompressed image (3). The quality of JPEG images is measured as a percentage of maximum, or on a scale of 0–12, the latter divided into quality categories of low (0–4), medium (5–7), high (8–9), or maximum (10–12). At settings of high or maximum, image degradation is virtually unnoticeable, but at medium becomes more apparent (4, with a setting of 6). At low settings quality becomes very noticeable (5, set at 3), and at the lowest, 0, images become virtually unusable (6).

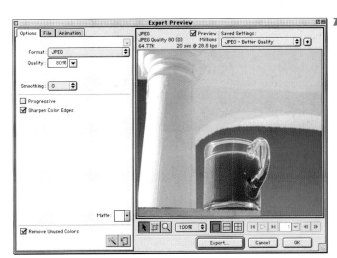

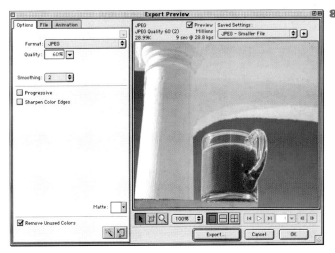

7

Good-quality JPEG images can still be quite compact—here, downloadable over a "standard" slow dial-up connection in 20 seconds. The image is sharp, with excellent color reproduction when viewed on a suitable system (one with more than 256 colors available).

8

Halving the file size, to download in only 9 seconds, has a significant effect on the sharpness, but little on the color. Given the transient nature of the Web, you need to ask yourself how long a viewer will study the image and what quality is needed, so you can choose the right compromise between download speed and quality. But by opting for JPEG, you run the risk of viewers with only 256 colors being disappointed by the rendering of the picture.

CONCENTRATED COLOR

GIF files use indexed color constrained to no more than 8 bits in depth (256 colors or less), making them ideal for safe color use. They employ a non-lossy compression method that is most effective when dealing with long runs of the same color horizontally along a row; vertical patterns, dithering, and anti-aliasing in the image will therefore result in larger file sizes.

Optional features that can be used in GIFs include interlacing and transparency, with or without an alpha channel. Interlacing is popular for those with slower Internet connections, as it shows a blurry preview image early during download, progressively gaining resolution. Transparency is effective for displaying non-rectangular images, and can either key to the background color (in which case you must avoid using that color in the heart of the image) or use an alpha channel.

Early concerns over parts of the GIF format that are covered by patents fueled the development of the PNG standard for color images 8, 24, or 32 bits deep. Although it is not supported by many browsers and does not work as well as JPEG on photographic images, it attempts to correct for the screen gamma.

1

Undithered GIF images can appear posterized, which, although occasionally attractive, are invariably undesirable, since perspective and clarity may be weakened, requiring you to soften edges between areas of solid color.

2

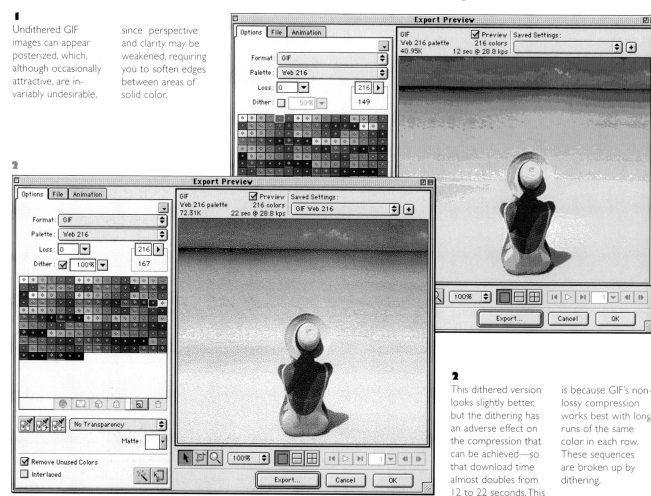

2

This dithered version looks slightly better, but the dithering has an adverse effect on the compression that can be achieved—so that download time almost doubles from 12 to 22 seconds. This is because GIF's non-lossy compression works best with long runs of the same color in each row. These sequences are broken up by dithering.

3

BoxTop's venerable PhotoGIF plug-in is a good way of optimizing GIF images in Photoshop. You are first prompted to correct the color palette.

4

Transparency and other options follow.

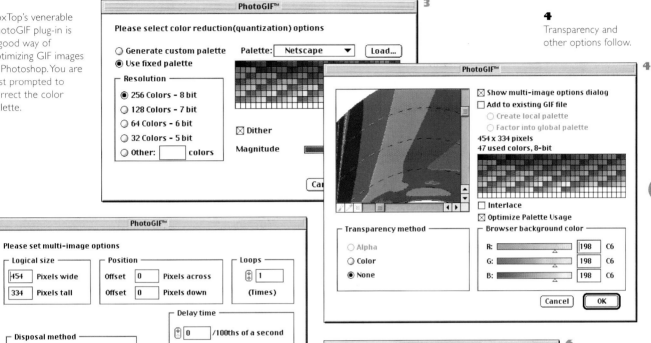

45

6

You can assemble GIF images into animations. These need to remain color-safe, too, unless you are intent on baffling your public with weird color effects.

6

For massive images, LizardTech's MrSID can squeeze megabytes into morsels of but a few kilobytes, using a patented lossy technique. This is best suited to large format scans (also, support is only via plug-in), so it remains a specialist option.

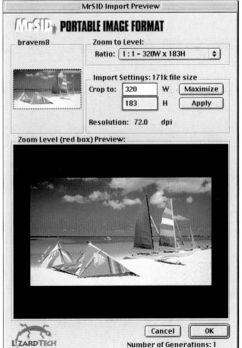

TESTING THE MARGINS

Given the contrasting approaches adopted by JPEG and GIF, you will not normally have difficulty deciding which is more appropriate. However, making the choice is not always easy, and cannot always be based on the nature of the picture and the expected download time. When preparing a number of similar pictures, experiment with one or two to see how well they work when compressed and then rendered, using the two methods. With JPEG in particular, try different levels of compression, and check the results at different color depths and on different systems.

If there is any risk that a browser will not be able to render a picture, give a clue as to what it is missing, using the ALT markup in HTML (essential if the image functions as key information, an active button—or, most of all, an image map, providing a text-only alternative). Badly rendered color is preferable to broken picture links, which could make your pages unusable.

46

1
This photograph is quite adequately rendered in just 256 colors, using an adaptive palette that is far from Web-safe. You might risk that palette on an Intranet where you know the browsers and hardware platforms, but it could suffer terribly in the hands of an old Windows 3 system.

2

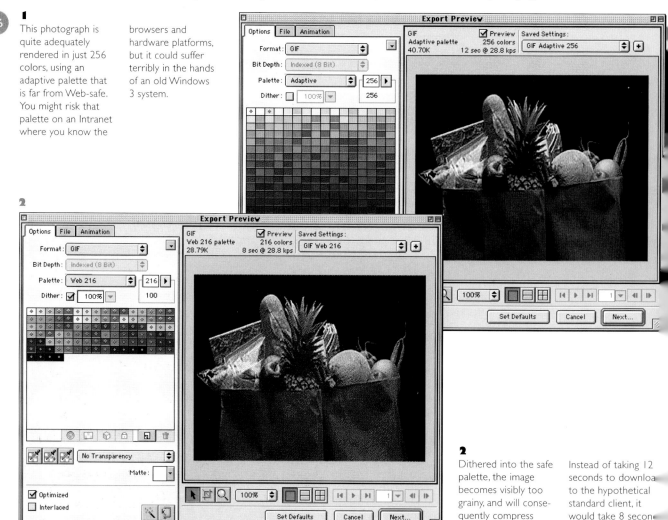

2
Dithered into the safe palette, the image becomes visibly too grainy, and will consequently compress relatively poorly. Instead of taking 12 seconds to download to the hypothetical standard client, it would take 8 second

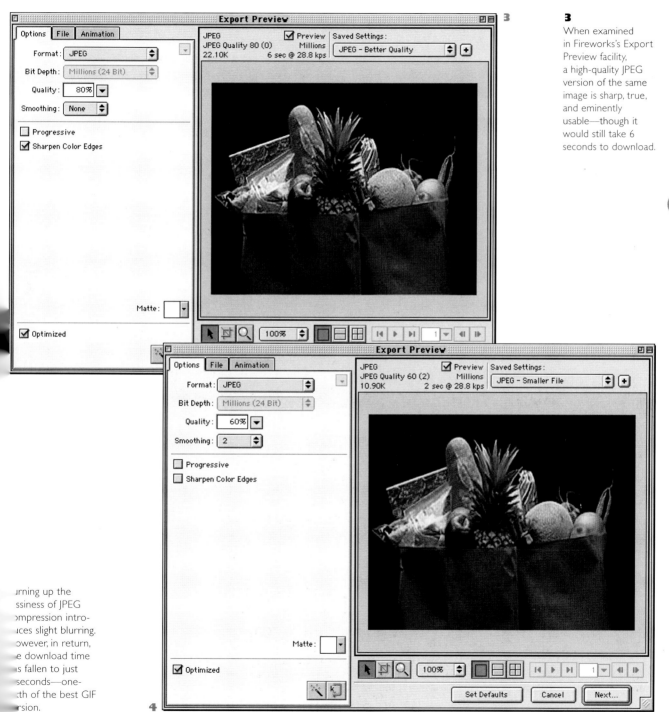

3

When examined in Fireworks's Export Preview facility, a high-quality JPEG version of the same image is sharp, true, and eminently usable—though it would still take 6 seconds to download.

...urning up the ...ssiness of JPEG ...ompression intro- ...uces slight blurring. ...owever, in return, ...e download time ...s fallen to just ...seconds—one- ...th of the best GIF ...rsion.

4

TONAL VARIATIONS

In contrast to printed media, continuous-tone mono-chrome images on the Web pose more problems than they solve. In the 216 safe colors, there are but four grays between black and white; even skillfully dithered, most images will look crude. Although much easier with a palette of 256 grays, all except six would be unsafe and could be rendered incorrectly on many monitors. Thus, high-quality monochrome work demands the full-color approach—so the attraction of potentially smaller file sizes is illusory.

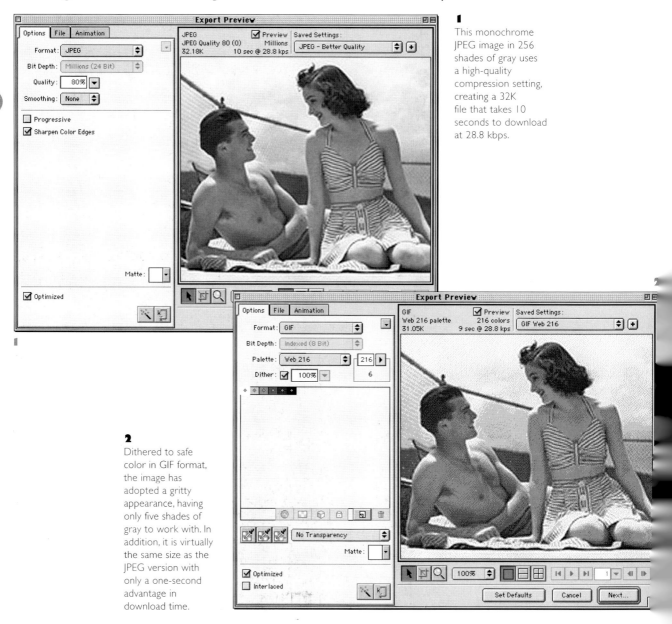

1
This monochrome JPEG image in 256 shades of gray uses a high-quality compression setting, creating a 32K file that takes 10 seconds to download at 28.8 kbps.

2
Dithered to safe color in GIF format, the image has adopted a gritty appearance, having only five shades of gray to work with. In addition, it is virtually the same size as the JPEG version with only a one-second advantage in download time.

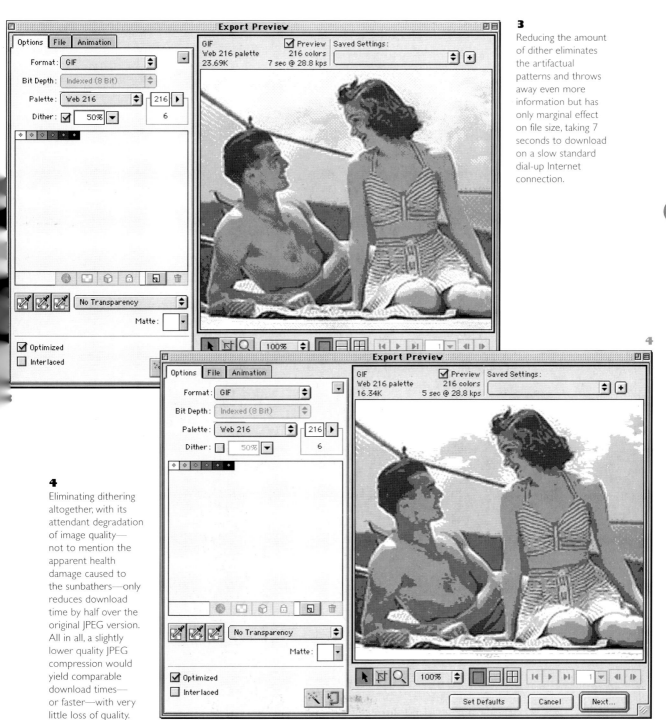

3
Reducing the amount of dither eliminates the artifactual patterns and throws away even more information but has only marginal effect on file size, taking 7 seconds to download on a slow standard dial-up Internet connection.

4
Eliminating dithering altogether, with its attendant degradation of image quality— not to mention the apparent health damage caused to the sunbathers—only reduces download time by half over the original JPEG version. All in all, a slightly lower quality JPEG compression would yield comparable download times— or faster—with very little loss of quality.

THROUGH A GLASS DARKLY

In the controlled and ordered printed medium, you wouldn't commit to print before satisfying yourself that proofs were up to the required standard and faithful in color reproduction. Electronic proofing for the Web requires that you view your finished pages on Windows and Mac OS (if not Unix/Linux) machines, using at least the two most popular browsers, Netscape Navigator and Microsoft Internet Explorer, in a range of different versions.

An immediately obvious difference will be between gamma values: while Windows systems usually operate at 2.2, Mac OS and most Unix boxes have a gamma less than 2.0 (as low as 1.7 on Silicon Graphics computers). Images that appeared balanced on a Mac are therefore going to appear darker when viewed in Windows. Alternatively, if you adjusted them to look right in Windows, then they will appear too light on a Mac. There is no easy solution, although the PNG graphics format attempts to perform gamma correction. Most designers end up working to a gamma of around 2.0 to 2.2, but this should be modified to take your most important users into account.

When performing electronic proofing, you need to check your pages at high and low color depths, typically 24-bit ("millions of colors") and 8-bit (256 colors). When restricted to 256 colors (the main reason for keeping to the Web-safe palette of 216), forced dithering can be much poorer than that achieved during design.

50

Viewed in Internet Explorer on a Mac, using the standard Mac gamma of 1.8, the detail in this rather dark picture looks fine.

2

This is how a Windows user, with a gamma of 2.2, would see the same picture—with detail beginning to disappear in the darker parts of the image. The picture should be adjusted so that it looks right at a gamma of around 2.0, the best compromise for a mixed audience.

PROOF POSITIVE

Printed versions of Web pages are potentially important records of your work, perhaps the only way of committing the ephemeral to more permanent form. However, you need to reverse the process commonly used to import images into Web pages: to achieve faithful reproduction, you must convert RGB images to CMYK. Although not easy on any system, ColorSync in the Mac OS is a clear advantage here, provided that you have built appropriate color profiles for your different output devices (your monitor and printer, at least).

Nor are Web browsers ideal applications from which to print. They struggle to hold sensible page sizes, and have suffered notorious bugs in the past. Web-authoring packages are not a good solution either, due to the limitations in their HTML rendering. Probably the best option currently available is to convert the relevant pages, or the complete Web site, into an Adobe Acrobat document and print that.

1 | 2 | 3
Unambitious page design (*1*) has its virtues when it comes time to print. The Disney page appears faultlessly on a mid-range color inkjet printer (*2*), and the inherent color contrast of the original helps it to survive even in black-and-white (*3*).

4 | 5 | 6
Under the same
conditions, the Jewel
page (4) breaks into
unappealing lumps
(5, 6) As usual in the
music business, if you
want a souvenir, you'll
have to buy the T-shirt.

PICTURE THIS

Now that the 2.7-million-pixel digital camera is no longer a novelty, there are more pixels floating around than can be decently used in a currently average Web image. The pictures on this page exaggerate the point, but we are still some way off being able to transmit large (and magnifiable) images across the Web.

1 | 2
The landscape (*left, with detail, above*) is a composite: the left-hand side comes fro a camera costing th same as a decent used family car— the right from one approximating the value of a reasonab meal for four peop The lower half of the image has beer sharpened, and enhanced with Aut Levels. The close-u shows obvious differences, but the browser window (reproduced at act size from a 1024 × 768 pixel screen) renders the whole scene virtually as c

3 | 4

Some after-treatment of the photographic image pays off. The original (3) was shot through a window clad with an amber anti-sun filter. Before producing JPEGs for screen use (4), a simple application of the Auto Curves filter cleaned up most of the color cast and lack of contrast. The JPEGs retain the skin tones reasonably well; only the GIF begins to show banding, though this is less offensive than the murky tones of the untreated half.

3

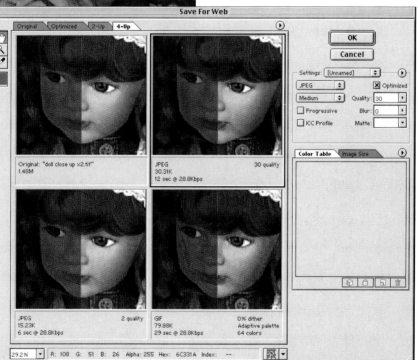

Save For Web

Original | Optimized | 2-Up | 4-Up

OK
Cancel

Settings: [Unnamed]

JPEG   ☒ Optimized
Medium   Quality: 30
☐ Progressive   Blur: 0
☐ ICC Profile   Matte:

Original: "doll close up x2.tif"
1.48M

JPEG   30 quality
30.31K
12 sec @ 28.8Kbps

JPEG   2 quality
15.23K
6 sec @ 28.8Kbps

GIF   0% dither
79.88K   Adaptive palette
29 sec @ 28.8Kbps   64 colors

Color Table | Image Size

29.2%   R: 108 G: 51 B: 26 Alpha: 255 Hex: 6C331A Index: --

4

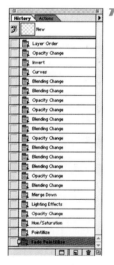

7

History | Actions

New
Layer Order
Opacity Change
Invert
Curves
Blending Change
Blending Change
Opacity Change
Opacity Change
Blending Change
Blending Change
Opacity Change
Blending Change
Blending Change
Blending Change
Opacity Change
Blending Change
Merge Down
Lighting Effects
Opacity Change
Hue/Saturation
Pointilize
Fade Pointilize

5 | 6 | 7

A perfectly reasonable photograph (5) can be submitted to the traditional Photoshop manipulations (6). The jury is out on whether these effects represent an improvement, but a fragment of the Photoshop History palette (7) gives an idea of the necessary maneuvers.

6

SWIMMING AGAINST THE TIDE

The business of threading colored images through the narrow eye of the file-size needle gets tedious at times. The pressure is always on to retain as much as possible of the quality of the original item. Or maybe not. There are opportunities to take advantage of the limitations of dither, GIF, and JPEG.

Whether you are using scanned images or digital photographs, like these, the apparently perverse first step is to ensure that the maximum amount of useful color information is retained. First, filters like Intellihance can be used to extract the maximum from the image; then creative degradation can begin.

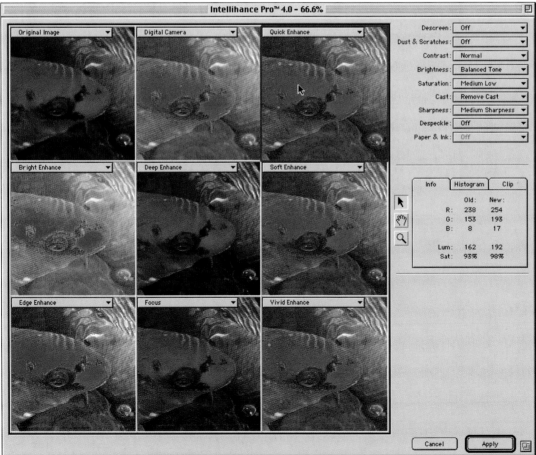

1 | 2
The original digital image (*1*) is treated in Intellihance to a number of variations (*2*). There are a further 14 available, each of which can be customized to suit a particular task.

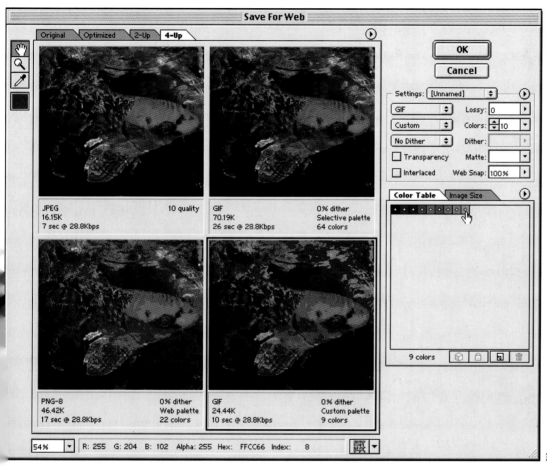

3 | 4 | 5 | 6
Photoshop's "Save for Web" command (3) offers an array of permutations before saving the image as a Web-ready document. The panel shows variations on the three available formats—the highlighted file demonstrates that the old adage about GIFs being no good for tonal images is only partly true. Farther below the surface (4), it is clear that dithering should not be dismissed out of hand. Application of Photoshop's Plastic Wrap filter (5) and an 8-color GIF palette leads to interesting effects. The same filter was used in conjunction with hue shifting (6) to finally lose touch with the original image.

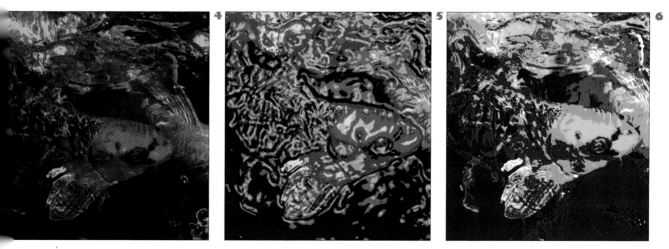

SCANNING FOR SCRAPS

Humble office scanners, so cheap that they may yet be given away with a box of cornflakes, nevertheless have great value in the relatively low-resolution environment of the Web. Flat subjects are obviously the norm, but even a rudimentary scanner has a surprisingly large depth of focus when faced with three-dimensional objects. Looking farther afield, the Web itself is a rich source of visual material—a lot for free, and much more if you're willing to use your charge card.

Even the screen itself can yield useful material for recycling. With the aid of a screen-capture utility and a good deal of dogged persistence, there are surprising effects to be realized.

60

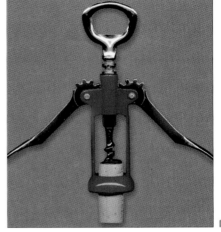

1
Try making a temporary paper tent over small objects like this corkscrew. With such metallic subjects, the moving scanner lamp will often oblige with curious reflections completely unlike the ones that are produced by conventional photography.

2 | 3 | 4 | 5 | 6
The default scanner setting (2) usually produces a weak result (4). Homing in on the required image (3) achieves better saturation (5). The same image on a digital camera (6) needs color balancing to retain the original chromolithograph's skin tones.

7 | 8 | 9 | 10 | 11
The Eclectic Artistry gallery is shown here to represent the thousands of such sites across the Web. Manet and Monet (9) would be proud to be in this popularizing company, and jealous of the automatic landscape production qualities of Bryce 3D (7). The stirring sky (11) is from a commercial photo CD. The two shapes (*far right*) are among many that are free to download from the USA's National Institute of Standards and Technology site; they are (8) a scanning electron micrograph of the charge at the tip of a roughness-measuring device, and (10) the damage caused by electrons to a fragment of biosensor film.

61

12
As a last resort, try grabbing bits of your own screen. This harmless collage (*left*) was made in Photoshop—entirely from screen captures of these two pages and the underlying desktop.

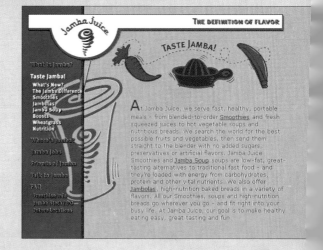

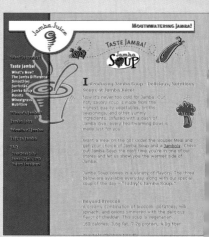

www.jambajuice.com

1 | 2 | 3 | 4

The Jamba Juices splash screen opens up with vibrant tropical-fruit-based colors that are opposite one another on the color wheel. The "wellennium planet" bursts open to reveal the "insides" of the site (1, 2). The strong purple of the opening screen is demoted for use in the opening text. On the following pages a pale-yellow background is selected to keep up the fruit-color theme—this color has the advantage of being neutral and of showing up the vivid purple of the text (3, 4). Text links, contrary to the received wisdom, are put into another fruit color—a bright orange. Raspberry red, tomato red, banana yellow, orange, and lime green maintain the fruit theme.

www.bridalbabe.com

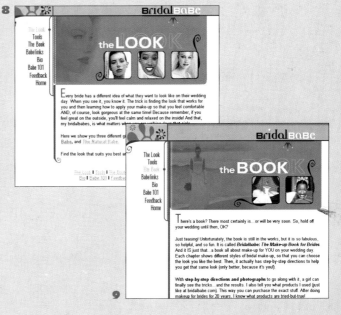

5 | 6 | 7 | 8 | 9
Bridal Babes uses a narrow range of allied colors, ranging from rose pink and fuchsia to lilac and lavender. These flowery hues help reinforce the atmosphere of ultrafemininity for the nuptial market. The principal drawback in the color scheme is that these warm colors tend to make the flesh tones look anemic. Liberal use of a white ground goes some way to balance out this effect. Curlicues and floral motifs evoke an earlier era when "babe" had a different meaning.

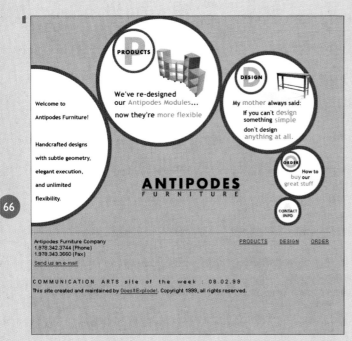

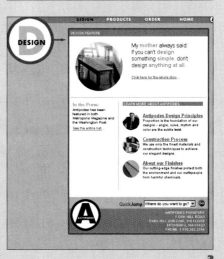

www.antipodesfurniture.com

1 | 2 | 3 | 4
Antipodes Furniture
restricts itself to a
very limited palette.
White, sage green,
and a narrow khaki
band make for a
cool and restrained
introduction. Product
shots are in mono-
tone at microscopic
sizes. The recurring
circular motif does
duty as a magnifying
lens to show off the
precision of the
furniture construction.
Solid, restrained
design is underlined
by the unattributed
quotation "My
mother always said 'If
you can't design
something simple,
don't design anything
at all,'" and by the
conservative black
and dark-blue type.
Subheads in the
HTML text are
colored to match the
restraint of the GIF-
based type.

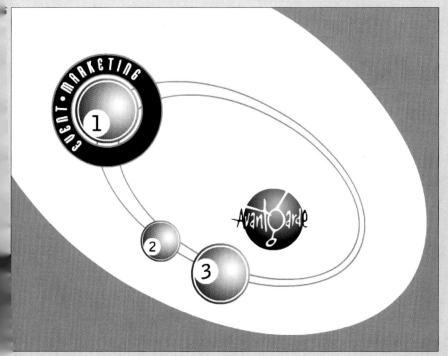

www.avantgarde.com

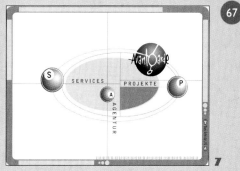

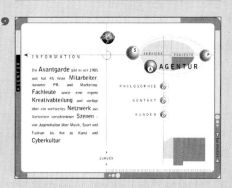

5 | 6 | 7 | 8 | 9

Understatement from the world of marketing and PR. What is going on here? This German site demands the Shockwave plug-in, and the little Macromedia banner makes clear the economy of color in the rest of the site. A shadow effect brings the frame forward; fine vertical lines create the illusion of a third color, which adds depth to the screen. Further interest is supplied by the engagingly willful use of a contrasting orange spot color in the subsequent frames.

68

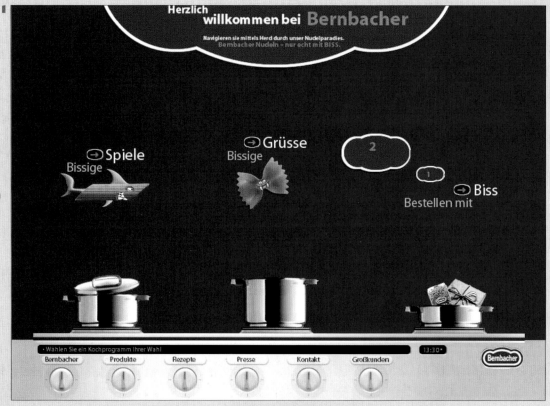

www.bernbacher.de

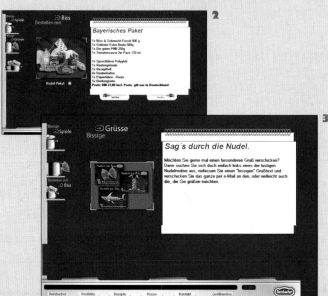

1 | 2 | 3

What can you do with dried pasta? Lots of interesting shapes but it is all pale yellow. The answer lies in the complementary color wheel—an ancient packaging designer had the right idea. Dark blue is the perfect foil to pale penne—shown here as hero, with the color contrast between dark blue and yellow making it look inviting. A *tour de force* of silvery-gray JPEGs glamorizes the cooking utensils.

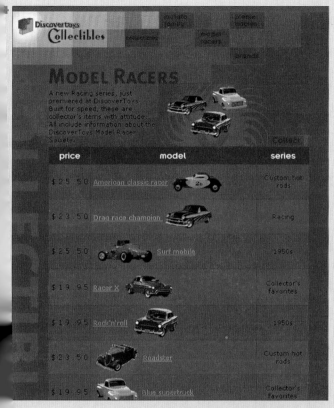

MODEL RACERS

A new Racing series, just premiered at DiscoverToys. Built for speed, these are collector's items with attitude. All include information about the DiscoverToys Model Racer Society.

price	model	series
$ 2 5 . 5 0	American classic racer	Custom hot rods
$ 2 3 . 5 0	Drag race champion	Racing
$ 2 5 . 5 0	Surf mobile	1950s
$ 1 9 . 9 5	Racer X	Collector's favorites
$ 1 9 . 9 5	Rock'n'roll	1950s
$ 2 3 . 5 0	Roadster	Custom hot rods
$ 1 9 . 9 5	Blue supertruck	Collector's favorites

Discovertoys Collectibles
Kids at Play Minds at Work

Remember that sticker album you had as a kid?

Collectibles offer a fascinating journey, bringing together past and future in an ever-evolving community. Collecting brings families and friends together with a shared appreciation of seeing related pieces become whole. Start your collection today...and watch this space for special offers later this summer!

DiscoverToys is an imaginary toy store Web site, designed and produced by 415 Productions demonstrating Macromedia products. It requires the latest Flash and Shockwave Players and doesn't actually allow you to buy things like a Mutato-Head (of course, you're encouraged to try).

69

MODEL RACERS

A new Racing series, just premiered at DiscoverToys. Built for speed, these are collector's items with attitude. All include information on the DiscoverToys Model Racer Society.

American classic

Limited edition of 150 models designed by artisan Bo Jones, inspired by the Unknown Racer archetype and (in part) by the Ford Prefect. Unique color, designed to reflect sunlight and white light so brightly that it appears to glow. 1/16 scale.

4 | 5 | 6 | 7

Warm and cozy on the Collectibles toys site; strong yellows and marigolds invite the viewer to linger in a reverie of real or imagined nostalgia. The blue of the text sings out to the prospective purchaser with an irresistible intensity.

MODEL RACERS

A new Racing series, just premiered at DiscoverToys. Built for speed, these are collector's items with attitude. All include information on the DiscoverToys Model Racer Society.

American classic racer

First edition of a new Racing series, just premiered at DiscoverToys. Built for speed, these are collector's items with attitude. Custom paint, has a scratch resistant coating, to protect it in actual play-race action. Includes information on the DiscoverToys Model Racer Society. Alternate Design.

www.discovertoys.com

1

Passion in a touch... perfection in a cup... summer in a spoon...One perfect moment.

WHAT'S NEW **Häagen-Dazs**

Buy an Ice Cream Heart Cake and Get a Free Tube of Frosting

What you write is none of our business! Get the details.

Send a Card from Monte Carlo

Or other dream destinations. Free International Moment e-cards are all new.

New! Ice Cream Flavours to Savour

Allow us to introduce new Créme Caramel Pecan and Mango ice cream.

New! Frozen Yogurt Flavours are Truly Tempting

Try Dulce de Leche and Strawberry frozen yogurt soon, and sigh.

Enter the world of **QUALITY** ice cream and see why we believe Häagen-Dazs is the finest. Sample our ice cream, sorbet, frozen yogurt and other wonderful **PRODUCTS**. Explore the magic of Häagen-Dazs at home with fine **SERVING IDEAS**. Find our **SHOPS & CAFES** around the globe. Look in on our **CLUBS** for offers available only to Häagen-Dazs devotees. Welcome.

GET PERFECT BYTES BY E-MAIL
News, ideas and other wonderful things via e-mail. Subscribe here.

JOIN THE PERFECT REWARDS™ PROGRAM
Special offers, new product news, and more by postal mail. (Available only in the U.S.)

VISIT THE HÄAGEN-DAZS JAPAN SITE

2 SERVING IDEAS

SERVING IDEAS

Häagen-Dazs is always remarkably comfortable at home. Whether you are serving yourself, planning an intimate dinner for two, or hosting a gathering, there is a Häagen-Dazs® ice cream, sorbet or frozen yogurt perfect for the moment. Try some of these serving and presentation ideas.

DESSERT RECIPES
DRINK RECIPES
PRESENTATIONS
GARNISHES
STORAGE AND SERVING

www.haagen-dazs.com

1 | 2 | 3

Häagen-Dazs is rightly feted in the annals of brand promotion for single-mindedness and devotion to core values. The name is a linguistic construct, at once vaguely Scandinavian (for the cool ice-cream values) and mysterious (for an exotic and luxurious feel). A vanilla background and a texture borrowed from the product packaging make a cool foil to the small and seductive ice-cream shots.

VING IDEAS

Dessert Recipes
Drink Recipes
Presentation
Garnishes
Storing and Serving

Dessert Recipes

BAKED ALASKAN SNOWBALLS
BISCOTTI PISTACHIO DESSERT
CAFFE MOCHA SEMIFREDDO
CHERRY SUNDAES IN CHOCOLATE MOUSSE SHELLS
CHOCOLATE 'N FRUIT PHYLLO TARTLETS
CHOCOLATE SHORTCAKE WITH STRAWBERRIES
CINNAMON MOCHA CREAM WITH TORTILLA CRISPS
COFFEE ALMOND ICE CREAM TORTE
COOKIE ICE CREAM-A-ROUNDS
CRANBERRIES 'N CREAM JUBILEE

GINGER PUMPKIN YOGURT PIE
HOLLY BERRY SUNDAE
LEMON RIBBON ICE CREAM PIE
MANGO SORBET WITH STRAWBERRY SAUCE
MOCHA HAZELNUT SYMPHONY
PEANUTTY ICE CREAM SANDWICHES
PINA COLADA PIE
PRALINE CREAM PUFFS
RASPBERRIES PEACHES 'N CREAM SHORTCAKE
REVEL BERRY ICE CREAM TORTE

4 | 5 | 6

The Scotch trade has thrived for decades on images of noble stags and club-room armchairs. Upstart drinks and changing tastes have begun to force a new attitude. Dewar's site plots a midway course, with lifestyle shots sitting on the warm and comforting cream of old. White Label, the flagship product, is recalled only in the page edges.

Dewar's promotes responsible drinking.
Dewar's, White Label and the Highlander Device are registered trademarks.
© 1999 Bacardi & Company Limited. Sole Distributor U.S. John Dewar & Sons Company, Miami, FL.
Blended scotch whisky - 40% Alc. by Vol.
View our Privacy Statement

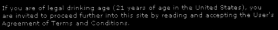

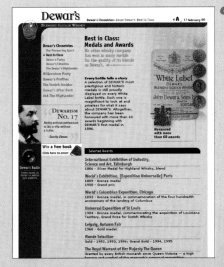

www.dewars.com

www.thefreedomtrail.org

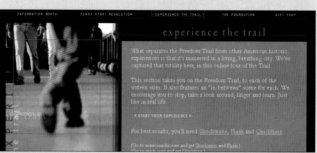

2

3

4

INFORMATION BOOTH   FIRST STOP: REVOLUTION   ‹ EXPERIENCE THE TRAIL ›   THE FOUNDATION   GIFT SHOP

the freedom trail

In 1958, the City of Boston was changed in the subtlest of ways.

A red line was painted on the sidewalk, starting at the Boston Common and going downtown, to the North End, then over the bridge to Charlestown and up to the Bunker Hill monument.

Sixteen historic sites, all significant in this country's early struggle for freedom, were connected by a 2.5 mile stripe that not only linked one place to another, but the past to the present.

Here we continue The Freedom Trail's history by introducing its first official Web site. Have a look around. We hope it encourages you to come visit.

1 | 2 | 3 | 4
The movie tradition is a great standby in the design of pages which are strongly photo-dependent. Colors appear more intense, and there is an illusion of better image sharpness. The Old North Church screen successfully breaks the oft-stated rule of not using white running text against a black background.

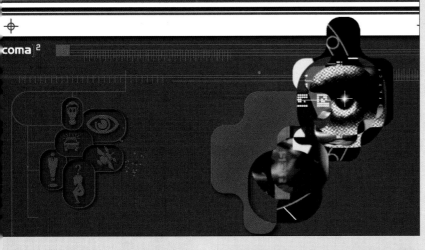

www.coma2.com

5 | 6 | 7 | 8 | 9

The Web artists of the Coma[2] site should know what they're doing. This virtuoso production has all the signs of confidence. The red (standard FF0000) kicks out against the lined green background.

Confident in the audience too—the assumption is that the viewers will all be equipped with 24-bit color. At lower resolutions, subtle shadow effects get minced by banding.

74

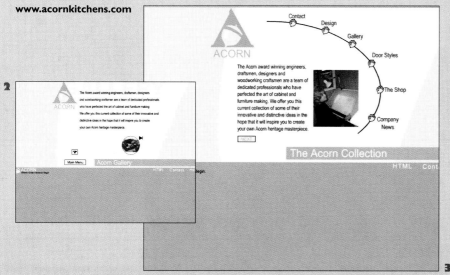

ACORN
Where Great Kitchens Begin.

HTML   Contact   Home

www.acornkitchens.com

1 | 2 | 3

The shock of the weak! The Acorn site color scheme is highly unusual, and appears to have taken inspiration from the desktop shot (3). Old folks with long memories will recall that almost all

drawing boards c in that curious gr exactly half-way between restful and nauseating. A precariously clam desk lamp lights t scene with a warr tungsten glow.

5

www.moet.com

6

|5|6|7

7

he Moët & Chandon
te uses a virtually
onochrome palette
ith the colors
elected echoing
930s photo chic.
he oatmeal suite is
eliberately chosen to
nt at the taste
the product—crisp,
y, and with a slightly
easty" taste. The

site contrasts with the
public perception of
a louder Moët &
Chandon, familiar to
us from thousands of
Grand Prix motor-
racing podia.
Chromatic restraint
and mannered type
make all the
difference here.

Thomas Feldmann

www.hirons.com

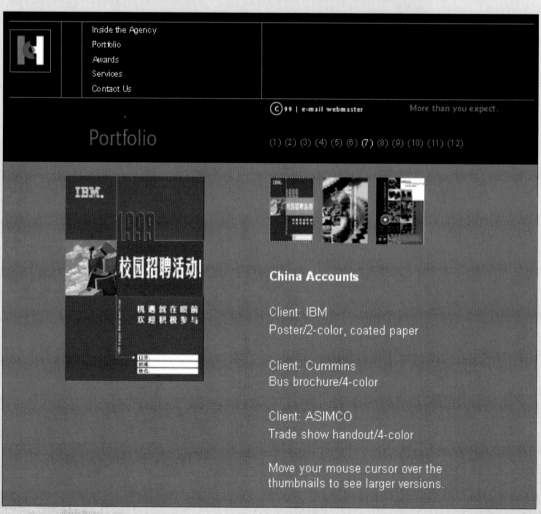

1 | 2 | 3
In the Hirons Agency site, an all-purpose industrial gray sets off a selection of colorful illustrations. The design rules are those of traditional corporate print—it's not hard to imagine these pages folded neatly in half with a wire stitch in the middle.

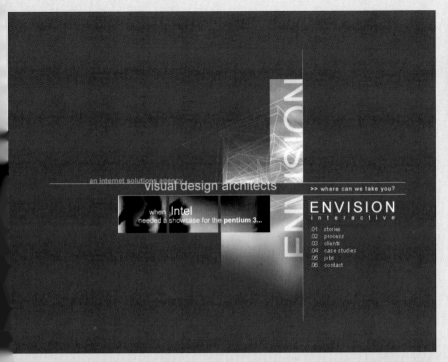

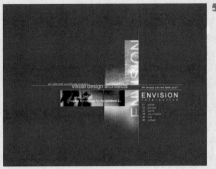

www.envisioninteractive.com

www.dennisinter.com

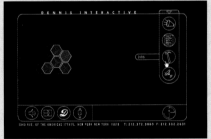

7

4 | 5 | 6 | 7

Two sites which stay in the strict confines of the monochrome palette, one with an airy photographic feel, the other sticking closely to street iconography. The Envision site (4, 5) stands up in low resolution, the soft graduations being inoffensively dithered (5). Dennis Interactive (6, 7) has no such concerns with a plain black ground and the benefit of the world's most well-known jeans tag. Finally, a question prompted by the Envision site: are Internet designers really architects? Or merely carpenters?

1

GABOR AG | CAREERS | THE PRESS | CONTACT | HOME | LINKS | LOTTERY | SHOP SEARCH

STYLE GUIDE

GABOR **Lady** GABOR **Trend / Fashion** GABOR **Jollys** GABOR **men**

Gabor

Click here !

**ATTENTION
NEW COLLECTION**

2

GABOR AG | CAREERS | THE PRESS | CONTACT | HOME | LINKS | LOTTERY | SHOP SEARCH

STYLE GUIDE

Lady

Wellness is ...

when the body and mind are in harmony. Gabor Lady is your first step to this feeling of well-being. Gabor shoes-with more width. Pleasant heels and comfortable equipping provide for special comfort. In more than 140 working steps, a pair of shoes with that certain extra is created from in some cases as many as 250 individual pieces. All you have to do is trust your good taste.

MODEL

Gabor

GABOR **Trend / Fashion** GABOR ▸**Lady** GABOR **Jollys** GABOR **men**

3

GABOR AG | CAREERS | THE PRESS | CONTACT | HOME | LINKS | LOTTERY | SHOP SEARCH

STYLE GUIDE

Exclusive for Gabor customers

Ever wondered about the right style for your personality?
Now's your chance to get it right.

Just answer the following questions honestly, and our stylist will counsel you with the last word on which shoes are absolutely you.

▶ Start here!

Gabor

I

4

GABOR AG | CAREERS | THE PRESS | CONTACT | HOME | LINKS | LOTTERY | SHOP SEARCH

STYLE GUIDE

Exclusive for Gabor customers

Lady

Ever wondered about the right style for your personality?   MODEL   NEXT
Now's your chance to get it right.

STYLE GUIDE

Just answer the following questions honestly, and our stylist will counsel you with the last word on which shoes are absolutely you.

▶ Start here!

Sporty Walking Shoe

Patent leather with crocodile embossing, comfortable width G, 30 mm heeled sole, Model 92.400.

Gabor

GABOR **Trend / Fashion** GABOR ▸**Lady** GABOR **Jollys** GABOR **men**

5

GABOR AG | KARRIERE | PRESSE | KONTAKT | HOME | LINKS | GEWINNSPIEL | SHOPSUCHE | ENGLISCH

TYPBERATUNG

GABOR **Lady** GABOR **Trend / Fashion** GABOR **Jollys** GABOR **men**

Gewinnen Sie mit Gabor !   Jetzt Neu

www.gabor.de

1 | 2 | 3 | 4 | 5

Skating deftly around some huge pitfalls, the Gabor site uses fancy footwork and a white background to make the screens look like familiar catalog pages. Low depth-of-field photography gives a hint of what the 3-D Web might offer one day. The resulting feather-edged images blend seamlessly with the pervasive white ground. Elsewhere, the visual material retreats even further (*above*) to form a ground for the real business of the site–consumer personal data collection.

6 | 7 | 8
In the Shoe History site's opening screen, the look of the 1910s is created using a limited-palette JPEG. This apparently monochrome image actually uses 21 different colors.

ww.centuryinshoes.com

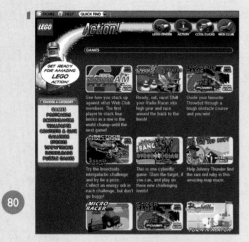

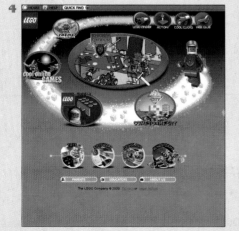

www.lego.com

1 | 2 | 3 | 4 | 5 | 6 | 7

Toy-box bright colors are the principal attraction of the Lego site. The Lego palette is extraordinarily well suited to the Web page. The addition of a few highlights lends an extra dimension to the screen and gives the feel of the toys themselves. The pages showing Lego's Star Wars merchandise (6, 7) employ the classic intergalactic background, a very economical GIF that is immediately recognizable.

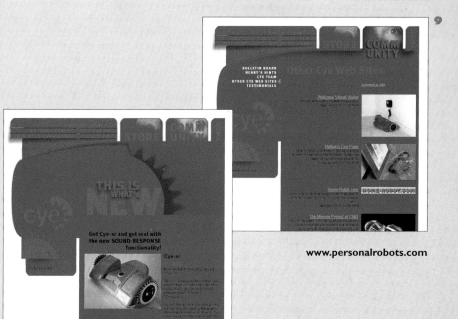

8 | 9 | 10

The Cye personal robots site is aimed equally at children and adults, and so avoids the toy-box palette. The robot products forcibly influence the colors and shapes of every screen element. Next step—the robot Web-page designer?

www.personalrobots.com

8

81

9

10

1

www.aids.at

2

3

1 | 2 | 3
The Austrian AIDS site shows elegance and restraint, both in its use of color and type. It neatly avoids the question of color association by going monochrome. There are many echoes he of the European tradition of political photomontage, but brought up to date with a striking panoramic page format.

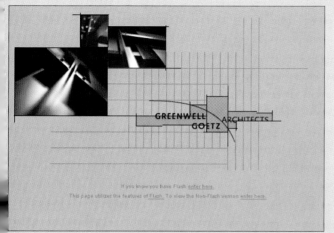

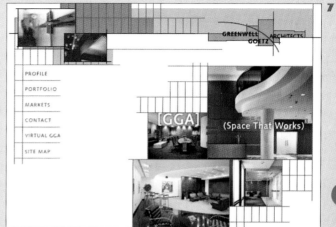

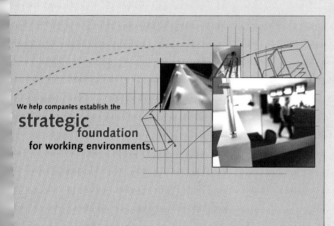

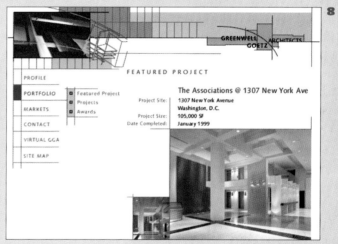

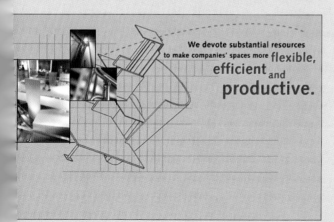

4 | 5 | 6 | 7 | 8

Greenwell Goetz Architects opts for a bookish look, with solid color used for the introductory "chapter opener" pages and white ground for the subsequent text-rich pages. Blueprint color photographs and "hand-drawn" sketches add to the studious atmosphere.

www.gga.com

84

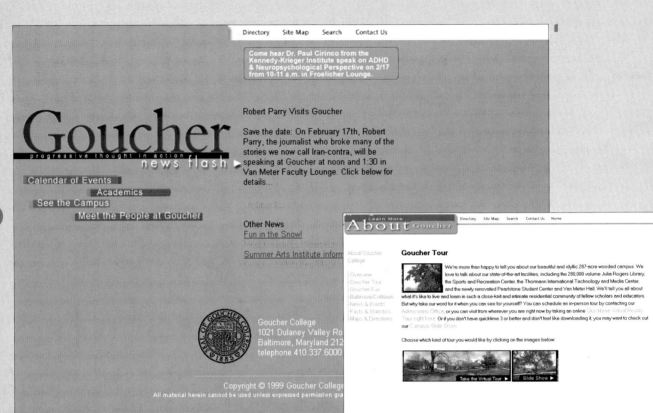

1|2|3

The Goucher and American Photography sites have very similar palettes. Both employ cool-blue back-grounds. The Goucher site has one additional blue and then starts to use green for text links and navigation; the text pages use black text against a white foreground. It has been deliberately made to look like a traditional college prospectus.

www.goucher.edu

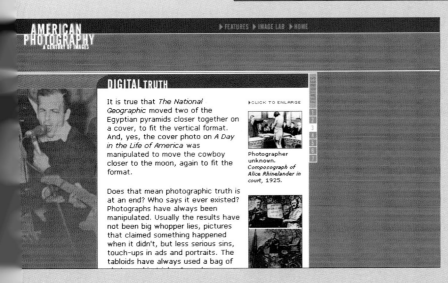

5

4 | 5 | 6

The prevailing style of "serious" US Web design is well represented by the American Photography site. It is a guide to a television series produced by the Public Broadcasting Service. Powder-blue and a highly contrasting orange are used in varying strengths to manage a multilayer presentation. Extra values are gained by lavish use of horizontal "scan lines" made of two colors. Served up as GIFs, these areas download at speed. The type hierarchy is also economically managed, using only combinations of blues and white.

www.pbs.org

www.clintbaker.com

1 | 2
Clint Baker has boldly
gone against the
received wisdom of
portfolio design. The
Wild West "Wanted"
poster look is created
out of a small brown
palette which looks
just as good dithered
as not. Even the text
links conform to the
leathery style.

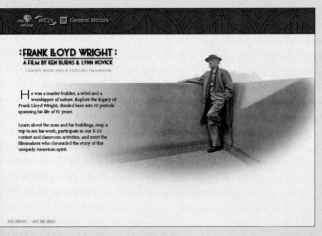

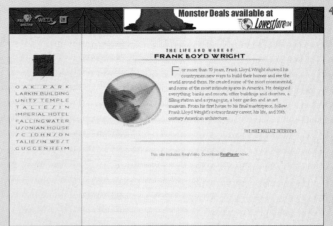

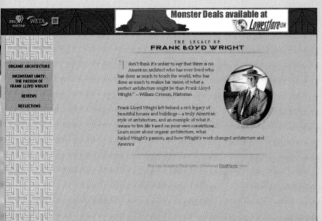

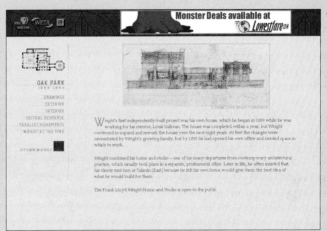

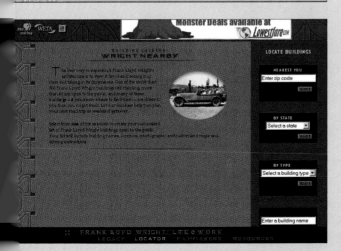

3 | 4 | 5 | 6 | 7

www.pbs.org/flw

The Frank Lloyd Wright biography site is a *tour de force* of feather-edge-GIF management. You might think a limited palette has been used, but the actual number of colors is surprisingly high— several browns have been employed to produce subtle graduations of color. The image stands up well to low-resolution dithering (though the crass advertising banner threatens to undo all the good work).

www.dataprotect.com

www.d2.com

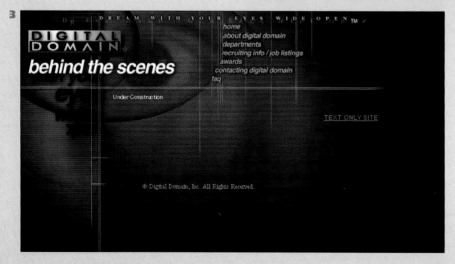

1 | 2

The Data Protect site is so subtle it is on the margins of invisibility. The illusion of monotone is given by a selection of very similar greens. The "rubbed out" look which recurs throughout the site deserves a fuller description—manuscript writers, when short of virgin parchment, used to scrape away at a previously used sheet. The fibers generally resisted such abuse and retained a trace of the original scribing. The technical term for this is palimpsest.

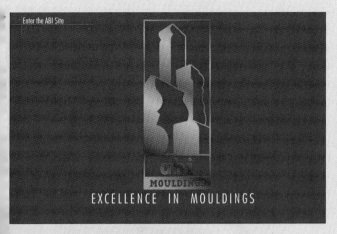

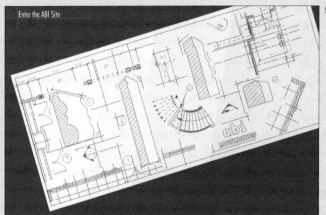

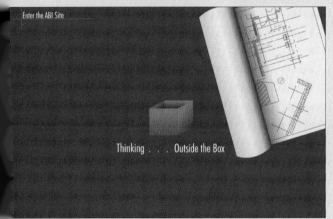

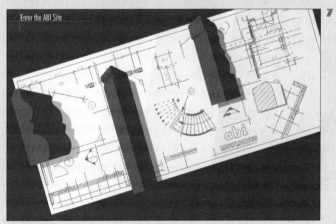

www.abimouldings.com

3 | 4 | 5 | 6 | 7 |

The Digital Domain site (3) is built up in somber background colors to show off their bright, sparky digital film effects work. The relevant part of the site was still under construction at the time of writing.

More dark colors are on display at the ABI Mouldings site (4, 5, 6, 7). This Flash-driven production has the molded sections springing to animated life out of blueprints. The bronze logo adds warmth.

1 | 2 | 3

Nigel Holmes, the British grand old man of US information graphics, veteran of 16 years' standing at *Time* magazine, launches himself upon the Web in primary colors. The junior school button icons demand to be clicked and reveal an impressive body of work in his inimitable style. It's a rare example of simple down-home graphics and cute drawing that actually works.

www.nigelholmes.com

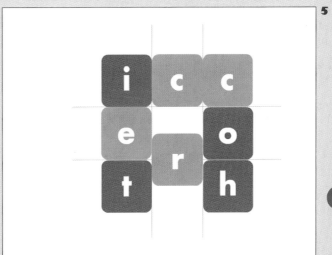

5

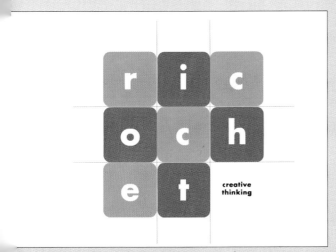

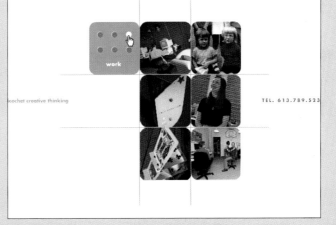

7

www.ricochetcreativethinking.ca

4 | 5 | 6 | 7
The Ricochet site works with Flash movies, and entices with an infuriatingly addictive version of the old sliding puzzle game. Powder blue and yellow are the colors of young, fresh, unfettered creative thinking. Well worth remembering.

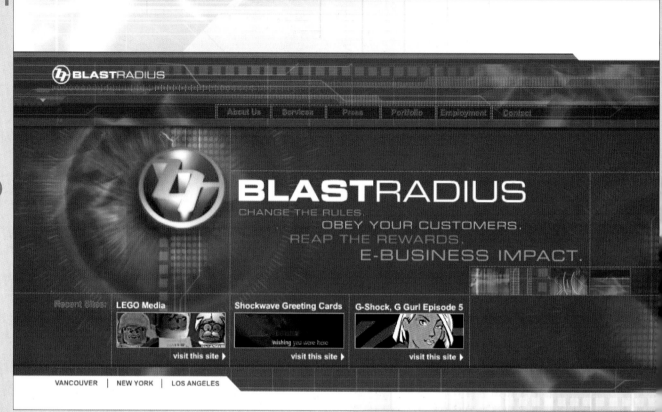

www.blastradius.com

1 | 2 | 3

Blastradius is a handy marker to symbolize Web design at the beginning of a new millennium. It is a synthesis of influence that stretch far back into science fiction magazines, futuristic literature, and plain old mechanical fantasy. The blue ligh suffusing the scene i borrowed from any alien horror movie c the 1960s, as are the trademark whirling vortices.

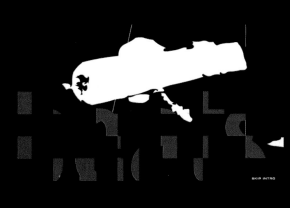

www.gshock.com

5

www.oneilleurope.com

|5|6|7

esigned by
astradius (*opposite*),
e G-Shock site (4,
comes in two
rsions—HTML and
xtreme." The latter
oice brings up a
sh movie with none
the parent site's
t-edged qualities.

O'Neill (6,7) hits the
spot for a boarding
and sailing site with
its blue, multilayered
and highly graduated.
Self-awareness is
neatly represented by
the designer's sticky
thumbprint at the
foot of the screen.

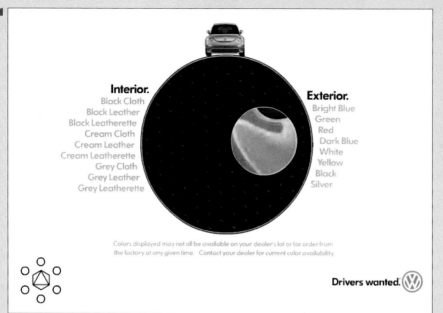

1

Interior.
Black Cloth
Black Leather
Black Leatherette
Cream Cloth
Cream Leather
Cream Leatherette
Grey Cloth
Grey Leather
Grey Leatherette

Exterior.
Bright Blue
Green
Red
Dark Blue
White
Yellow
Black
Silver

Colors displayed may not all be available on your dealer's lot or for order from the factory at any given time.   Contact your dealer for current color availability.

Drivers wanted.

3

Interior.
Black Cloth
Black Leather
Black Leatherette
Cream Cloth
Cream Leather
Cream Leatherette
Grey Cloth
Grey Leather
Grey Leatherette

Exterior.
Bright Blue
Green
Red
Dark Blue
White
Yellow
Black
Silver

Colors displayed may not all be available on your dealer's lot or for order from the factory at any given time.   Contact your dealer for current color availability.

Drivers wanted.

www.turbonium.com

1 | 2 | 3 | 4

The Volkswagen site has the look of traditional VW press advertising—a simple image of the car, a white ground, and a pay-off slogan, all in the house Futura face. Color is the point here, and accurate color at that. The viewer is able to test all the available paint and trim variations, choose features, and proceed all the way to just short of purchase. Some of the new Beetle colors are unusual, so a dealer visit is advised to check the browser's view.

6

5

95

7

8

www.chryslercars.com

9

5 | 6 | 7 | 8 | 9

The Chrysler car (a 1930s retro wagon) is the hero. Black always made cars look good, and the profound black of a well-adjusted monitor makes them look even better. On this site as well you can try out vehicle colors—the browser takes a few moments to render the smart silver original into a rather less desirable Deep Cranberry Pearl Coat.

1

new & notable
intro to the classics
concert calendar
box office
virtual visit
carnegie then & now
support the hall
learning center
gift shop
services guide
mailing list

MAIN MENU

© CHC 1996-2000

2

Timeline™

The story of Carnegie Hall begins with Leopold Damrosch (at right with son Walter), who left Germany in 1871, bound for America. Within two years, he had organized the Oratorio Society and, by 1877, he founded the New York Symphony Society. His new organizations did not have a permanent home and so he began to search for a location and money to build New York City's first large concert hall. Leopold died in 1885, leaving the direction of his two musical organizations and his dream of a concert hall to his 23-year-old son, Walter. Walter found his patron in steel tycoon Andrew Carnegie, a member of the Oratorio Society's board. By 1887 Damrosch had won Carnegie's support for a concert hall, and Carnegie began searching for a location.

3

WELCOME TO
CARNEGIE
HALL

main menu

1 | 2 | 3
The Carnegie Hall
site uses a color
combination straight
out of the formal
artist's wheel. A rich
dark blue, evocative
of luxury, pleasure,
and a concert hall
atmosphere, is used
for the background
color. This shows up
the gold and red of
the inset pictures
vividly. The orange
of the main text
headings coordinates
with the rollovers.
A clean white
background supports
the text-heavy scroll
of artists who have
appeared at Carnegie
Hall. James McNeill
Whistler, who made a
nocturne out of this
very combination of
colors, might be
accorded a late entry
into the Carnegie
Hall of Fame.

www.carnegiehall.com

4 | 5 | 6 | 7

The New York SoHo site demonstrates the way of the new cartography. The names of the stores on West Broadway are plotted in the right geographical place; those with Web sites have clickable links. The choice of a dark green background forces a revision of the link color conventions. Taking a cue from the traffic signals, life is red, style is yellow, and art is green. Enterprises unequipped with links are relegated to the dullest of grays.

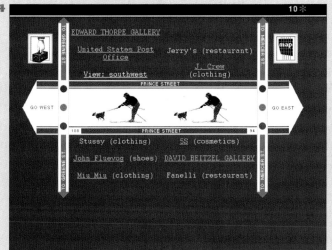

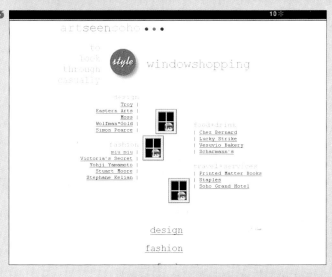

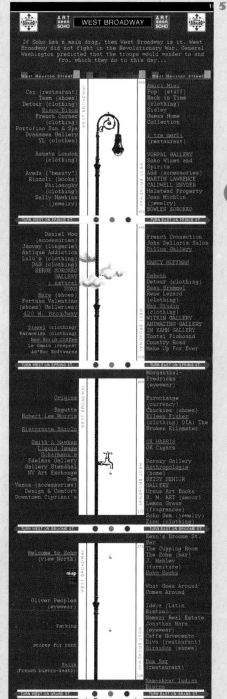

www.artseensoho.com

98

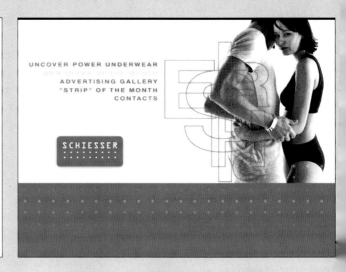

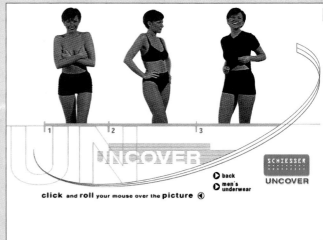

1 | 2 | 3 | 4

Power underwear was always going to be a tough assignment, and this pitch by the Coma² agency makes a brave attempt. The microscopic token man in the opening screen, though clad in a monochrome mackintosh, is no deviant onlooker. Powered by QuickTime, he disrobes along with the girls. Flesh tones look good against a white ground, and blue has no sinister associations, so the look is of a clean, wholesome catalog page.

www.coma2.com

6

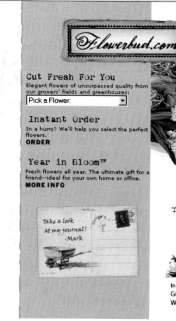

99

7

9

|6|7|8|9

The flowerbud.com site offers a solution to any online florist's conundrum—the natural desire to show every flower in its true colors at life-size is frustrated by the limitation of file size. Small color images in well-judged hues draw the buyer in. The background with a faded-out green flower image is evocative of the palely printed wrapping paper traditionally used at the old-style florist's bench.

www.flowerbud.com

1

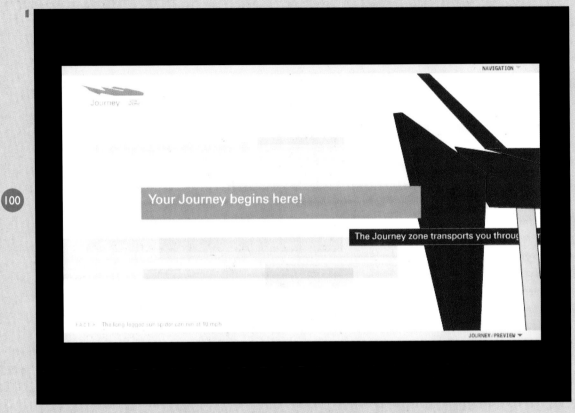

1 | 2 | 3 | 4

This Flash-driven site promoting the Ford installation moves along at a cracking pace. One of the virtues of the Flash application is that it encourages simpler and reductive design processes. Though the temptations of over-elaboration are still present, the demands of orchestrating animation as well as shape seem to lead to more elegant solutions. On the occasions where they don't, at least it's all over fairly quickly.

2

3

www.journey.ford.co.uk

4

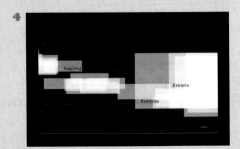

5 | 6 | 7 | 8 | 9 | 10 | 11

The first five screens of the Cool Films site show an economy of both color and style. But the black-and-white drawings are not only stylistically simple; they offer the simplest way of getting a moving image on screen. In the last two frames, reference is made to early pop videos. Screen (10), with its vibrant yellow border (waving a fond goodbye to naturalistic color), owes a large debt to Jamie Reid's Sex Pistols artwork.

www.coolfilms.com

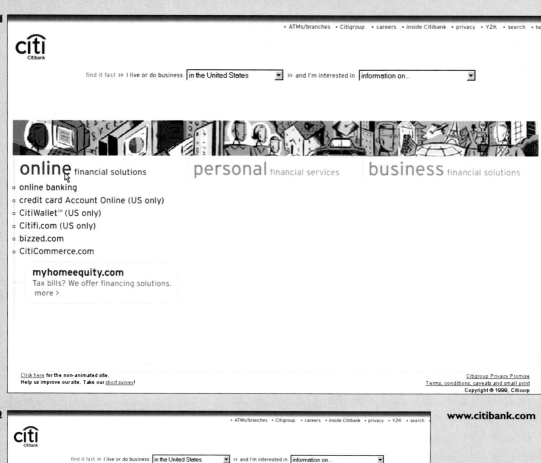

1 | 2
Deliberately styled like an online version of the corporate brochure, the Citibank site is fitted with simple rollovers which reveal selected sections in turn. The frieze graphics are in the tradition of the reassuringly naive style favored by financial institutions to achieve the customer-friendly look. Warm colors liven up the chosen topic— just remember that overdrafts were, are, and always will be red.

www.citibank.com

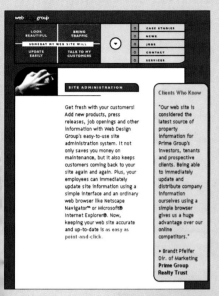

SITE ADMINISTRATION

Get fresh with your customers! Add new products, press releases, job openings and other information with Web Design Group's easy-to-use site administration system. It not only saves you money on maintenance, but it also keeps customers coming back to your site again and again. Plus, your employees can immediately update site information using a simple interface and an ordinary web browser like Netscape Navigator™ or Microsoft® Internet Explorer®. Now, keeping your web site accurate and up-to-date is as easy as point-and-click.

Clients Who Know

"Our web site is considered the latest source of property information for Prime Group's investors, tenants and prospective clients. Being able to immediately update and distribute company information ourselves using a simple browser gives us a huge advantage over our online competitors."

» Brandt Pfeifer
Dir. of Marketing
**Prime Group
Realty Trust**

CASE STUDIES

Company
Allied Vans

Industry
Transportation and Relocation Services

Application
Web site re-design

Description
Allied Van Lines is the world's leading moving services company. The interface design enables Allied Van Lines to be

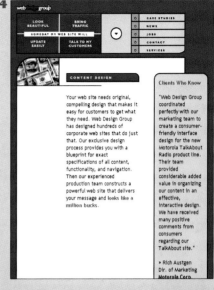

CONTENT DESIGN

Your web site needs original, compelling design that makes it easy for customers to get what they need. Web Design Group has designed hundreds of corporate web sites that do just that. Our exclusive design process provides you with a blueprint for exact specifications of all content, functionality, and navigation. Then our experienced production team constructs a powerful web site that delivers your message and looks like a million bucks.

Clients Who Know

"Web Design Group coordinated perfectly with our marketing team to create a consumer-friendly interface design for the new Motorola TalkAbout Radio product line. Their team provided considerable added value in organizing our content in an effective, interactive design. We have received many positive comments from consumers regarding our TalkAbout site."

» Rich Austgen
Dir. of Marketing
Motorola Corp.

103

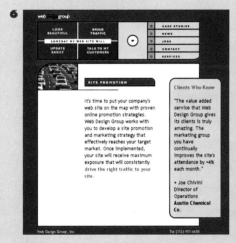

SITE PROMOTION

It's time to put your company's web site on the map with proven online promotion strategies. Web Design Group works with you to develop a site promotion and marketing strategy that effectively reaches your target market. Once implemented, your site will receive maximum exposure that will consistently drive the right traffic to your site.

Clients Who Know

"The value added service that Web Design Group gives its clients is truly amazing. The marketing group you have continually improves the site's attendance by ~4% each month."

» Joe Chivini
Director of Operations
Austin Chemical Co.

Web Design Group, Inc.   Tel (312) 951-6688

3 | 4 | 5 | 6 | 7

Friendly style also at the Web Design Group. A simple logic—choose four colors and employ each one as a highlight color in a dependent window.

The navigational device also unifies the text pages. The use of a themed color graphic at the top left of each page adds interest to flat tints.

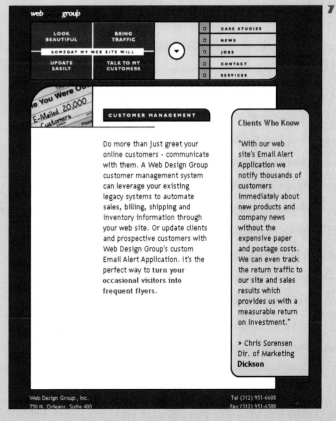

CUSTOMER MANAGEMENT

Do more than just greet your online customers - communicate with them. A Web Design Group customer management system can leverage your existing legacy systems to automate sales, billing, shipping and inventory information through your web site. Or update clients and prospective customers with Web Design Group's custom Email Alert Application. It's the perfect way to turn your occasional visitors into frequent flyers.

Clients Who Know

"With our web site's Email Alert Application we notify thousands of customers immediately about new products and company news without the expensive paper and postage costs. We can even track the return traffic to our site and sales results which provides us with a measurable return on investment."

» Chris Sorensen
Dir. of Marketing
Dickson

Web Design Group, Inc.
750 N. Orleans, Suite 400

Tel (312) 951-6688
Fax (312) 951-6588

www.webdesigngroup.com

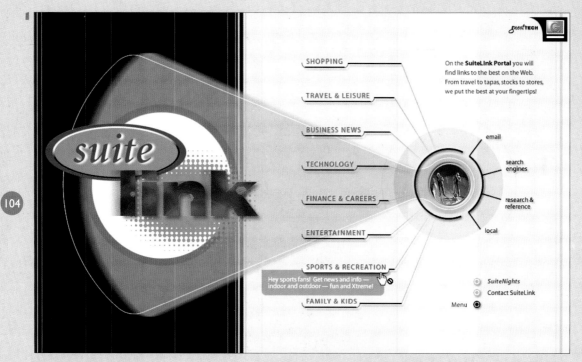

SHOPPING

TRAVEL & LEISURE

BUSINESS NEWS

TECHNOLOGY

FINANCE & CAREERS

ENTERTAINMENT

SPORTS & RECREATION

Hey sports fans! Get news and info — indoor and outdoor — fun and Xtreme!

FAMILY & KIDS

On the **SuiteLink Portal** you will find links to the best on the Web. From travel to tapas, stocks to stores, we put the best at your fingertips!

email

search engines

research & reference

local

SuiteNights

Contact SuiteLink

Menu

1 | 2 | 3
Image slicing gives a sophisticated 3-D appearance to Suite Link's opening page. A cornucopia of effects, such as white drop shadows, imitation halftone dot patterns, and shadowed leader lines, is displayed in this screen. On subsequent pages the pastel background throws the Suite Link logo into sharp relief. The transparency effect has been handled skillfully.

www.suitelink.com

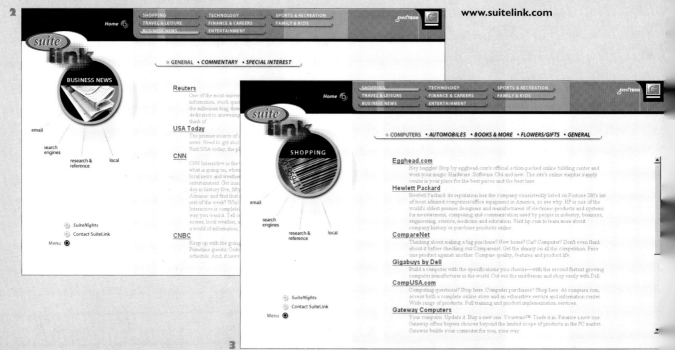

104

4 | 5 | 6

In the William B site, top and bottom bands of deep pink draw attention with their brashness, making the bold statement that the clothes and design can stand up to the assault of deep pink. Less assured operators would retreat to the gloomier reaches of "DimGray."

WILLIAM B

Inspired by Fendi's handbags,
this heavy cotton skirt has a
silk trimmed waistband, full silk lining
and **generous beaded fringe.**

Portobello Skirt

Welcome to williamb.com!

Check out the latest William B. styles by clicking on the roman numerals to the left.

Head back and click on any of the letters above to get the scoop on William B., find out our retail locations, get the skinny on who's wearing William B. and what the press is saying; and best of all, an exclusive sneak peak at what William B. is planning for next season.

Or you can always just play around with our fabulous color changer below.

Don't forget to e-mail us, join the William B. mailing list and tell us what you think of all this!

wb@williamb.com

105

i *ii* *iii* *iv* *v*

WILLIAM B

This strapless dress is made
of **supple velvet,** has long fringe
at the hem line and
is tailored to fit **exquisitely.**

Red Velvet Dress

Welcome to williamb.com!

Check out the latest William B. styles by clicking on the roman numerals to the left.

Head back and click on any of the letters above to get the scoop on William B., find out our retail locations, get the skinny on who's wearing William B. and what the press is saying; and best of all, an exclusive sneak peak at what William B. is planning for next season.

Or you can always just play around with our fabulous color changer below.

Don't forget to e-mail us, join the William B. mailing list and tell us what you think of all this!

wb@williamb.com

www.williamb.com

WILLIAM B

Made of **sheer, lightweight wool,**
this orange sweater has
three-quarter length sleeves
and a **slim tailored fit.**

Sheer Wool Sweater

1

www.martini.com

2

supported by
V•X Ally McBeal

3

1 | 2 | 3

Martini is riding high on the wave of 1970s retro chic. Strong bands of colors are set off by soft shades of gray. Looking nostalgically down into the colors of the cocktail glasses stimulates memories of ill-advised T-shirts. This largely wordless site encourages idle mouse-clicking on randomly presented images—just the thing for the happy hour.

DON'T FOOL. KEEP COOL.

ARNOLD ANDRÉ CIGARS

Independence

Specials

Screensaver

Gästebuch

Kontakt

Fine cigar INDEPENDENCE

www.independence-cigar.de

MO
SF MA
SAN FRANCISCO MUSEUM OF MODERN ART
VISIT INFO CALENDAR EDUCATION MEMBERSHIP SHOP EXHIBITIONS COLLECTIONS E-SPACE
SEARCH > SFMOMA

SFMOMA Webby Prize Awarded Work   Formula May 19, 2000   Rebellissance Ball June 24, 2000

www.sfmoma.org

4 | 5

107

Farther back, this time, to the heights of 1940s US military chic with the Independence Cigar Company (4). The blue-chinned pilot epitomizes the fearless bravery of flying and tobacco. Pipe-smoking Belgian René Magritte is celebrated at the San Francisco Museum of Modern Art for his 1953 *Golconda* (5). His description of the process of picture-making could stand equally for Web-page design: "They evoke mystery. . . when one sees one of my pictures, one asks oneself the simple question 'What does it mean?'—it does not mean anything, because mystery means nothing either. It is unknowable."

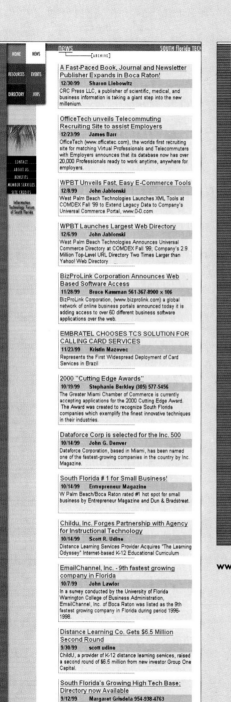

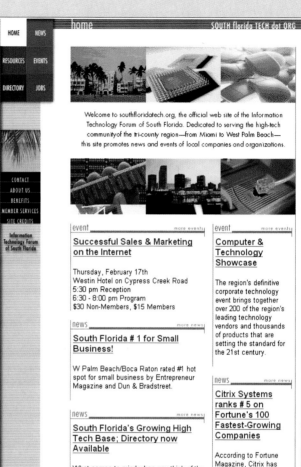

1 | 2

The pages from the South Florida Technical Data Organization demonstrate how to control texture and tone by the skillful manipulation of bands of color in a limited palette. More elevated information-heavy enterprises could learn from the understated clarity of this site.

www.southfloridatech.org

4

6

109

5

8

9

3 | 4 | 5 | 6 | 7 | 8 | 9

The Elixir Studio site map deliberately looks like a subway map. Very self-referential, as this design group specializes in transport graphics. They have their fingers in other graphic pies as well, with machine images and violent color contrast.

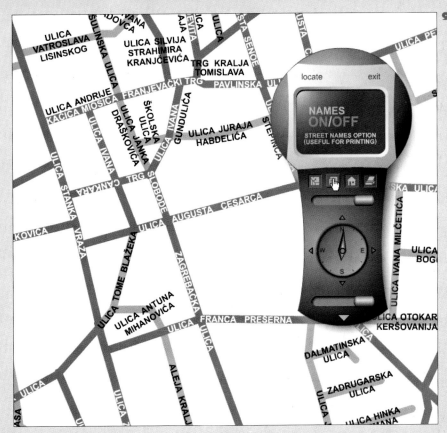

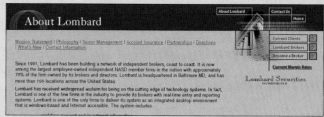

www.golombard.com

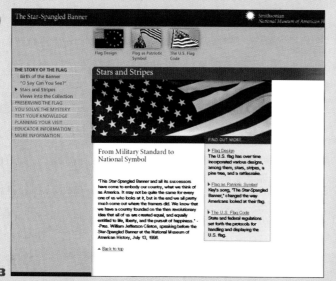

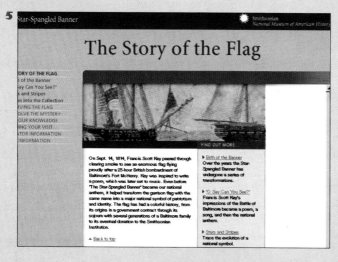

1 | 2 | 3 | 4 | 5 | 6 | 7 | 8

The green ("dark khaki") background selected for these sites is rarely seen in print—it is rather muddy and difficult to render attractively. On the Web, however, it has come to denote scholarship and wholesomeness (lots of museum sites use it). The Walrus site (6, 7, 8) makes great use of this potentially mucky end of the spectrum, with a cheerful yellow for emphasis.

www.americanhistory.si.edu

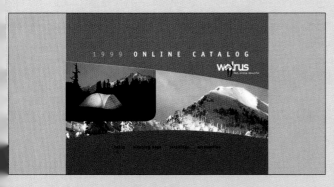

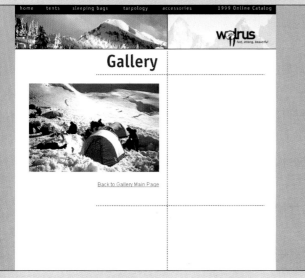

Gallery

Back to Gallery Main Page

CLICK HERE ▶

4 Season Technical

Backpacker

Active Family

POLE SLEEVES

SEAM-TAPING

GROMMETS

QUIET ZIPPER PULLS

QUIET ZIPPER PULLS

Our quiet zipper pulls of braided cord and plastic tabs that are large and easy to use - even with gloves on.

QUIET ZIPPER PULLS

GROMMETS

GROMMETS

Made in the U.S. out of solid brass, our spur grommets are as tough as they get. With multiple grommets on each strap you are guaranteed a tight pitch.

Go ahead and keep your expectations high.

You expect a lot when you buy a tent - and you should. We design and build our tents with the assumption that you demand the best possible design, materials and functionality that you can find in a tent. Then we make them affordable. So, whether you are looking for extra storage to keep your gear dry, or storm worthiness to keep you dry, you are going to find Walrus meets your needs - all at a cost that won't bleed your wallet dry.

▶ TENT FINDER

THE TENT

While the flysheet is the roof over your head, the tent body is your living room. You want your living room to be nice and dry, with no intrusive insects, and your tent should be too. With a Walrus there is room to store things, room to fully sit up*, lie down easily to sleep or to stargaze, and the ability to control ventilation. The basic comforts are always there in a Walrus tent.

* the ultra-light series may not accommodate sitting up

VENTILATION

Our large doors, expansive windows and strategically placed "eyelid" vents insure maximum airflow for the ultimate control in ventilation.

VENTILATION

VESTIBULES

VESTIBULES

Large and well-ventilated, our pole-supported vestibules offer extra protection from the elements.

CONTROLLABLE VENTS

Our new "eyelid" vents increase your control over tent ventilation.

CONTROLLABLE VENTS

FIELD REPAIRABLE POLES

Our tent poles are some of the strongest in the industry - Extruded from 7001 Hi-tensule aluminum, our poles are annodized for protection from the elements. The shock-corded, locking tip assures a secure connection for a tightly pitched tent. With a pole this strong it is easy to understand how we can guarantee them for life.

FIELD REPAIRABLE POLES

FLYSHEETS

Our rainflys are made of an exclusive blend of polyester and nylon, in a weave we call Diamondback™. This combination resists UV degradation better than nylon alone, and is more dimensionally stable, providing less sag when wet and less shrinkage when hot. Flysheets are cut to fully protect the tent by coming down low to the ground, while leaving space for airflow to come up and under the fly, helping prevent condensation build-up. Set-up is a breeze with guypoints that attach to the tent frame, and easy to use side-release buckles that fasten to the treated, non-wicking, stake-out webbing. Care is taken to pattern and cut the rainfly, so it will taut to quickly shed rain.

GEARLOFTS & STORAGE POCKETS

We've all scrambled to find our flashlight under the seas of sleeping bags and gear in our tent, but with our handy and unobtrusive gear lofts and storage pockets, everything will be in easy reach.

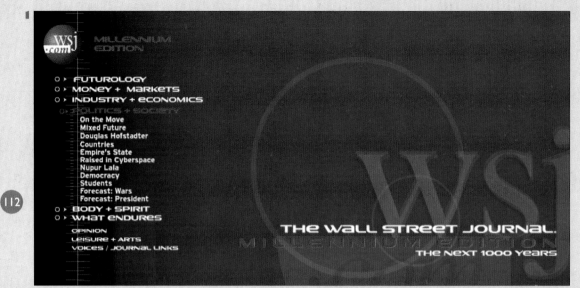

www.interactive.wsj.com

1

The *Wall Street Journal* has long had a strong presence on the Internet. Drop shadows here give a "carved in stone" effect—suitable for a paper that firmly believes it will be around for the next 1,000 years. The broad graduated background, however, gets badly dithered in low-end browsers.

2 | 3

The Audemars Piguet opening screen benefits from assured image control in the way the background color has invaded the central image. The dominant green color is picked up in the background of the subsequent screen.

www.audemarspiguet.com

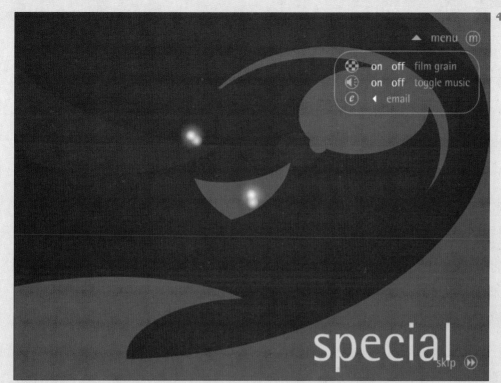

4 | 5
This site shows the
use of two close
colors to create witty
illusion. Which is the
figure and which is
the ground? They
appear to change
places seamlessly.

113

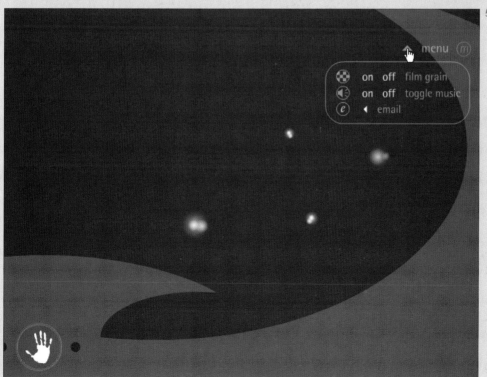

5

114

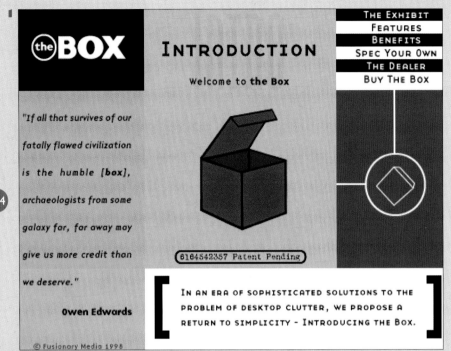

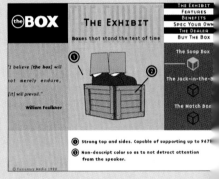

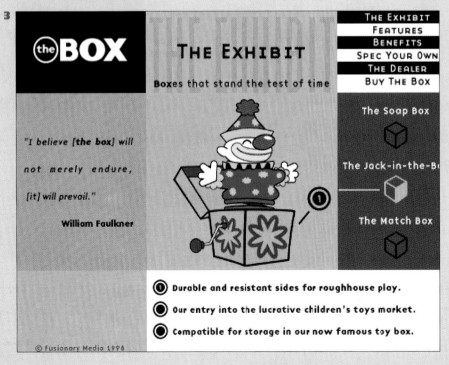

1 | 2 | 3 | 4 | 5 | 6 | 7 | 8 | 9

An object lesson in gaining attention and memorability through the use of color and contrast. The format remains consistent across the whole site; only the color blocks change. Three colors are used on each page, along with black and white; and the colors selected are shades of each other. Note the subliminal repetition of the page title on the background of the central panel, in the midtone of the three colors selected. You may hate it, the box, as well as the T-shirt, but you'll never forget it.

www.sixsides.com

Panel 1

the BOX

BENEFITS

Why you should own **the Box**

THE EXHIBIT
FEATURES
BENEFITS
SPEC YOUR OWN
THE DEALER
BUY THE BOX

"Dost thou love life? Then do not squander [the box], for that is the stuff life is made of."

Benjamin Franklin

Organization

Compatibility

Image

1. Handy storage for personal items and office tools.
2. Free up valuable desk space - eliminate clutter.
3. Coming soon: peekaboo window for easy viewing of box contents.

Panel 2

the BOX

THE DEALER

Your exclusive source for **the Box**

THE EXHIBIT
FEATURES
BENEFITS
SPEC YOUR OWN
THE DEALER
BUY THE BOX

"The measure of a man is what he does with [the box]."

Pittacus

About the Dealer

Dealer Location

Contact the Dealer

1. Engineering and Design Shop:
2. Manufacturing Facility:
3. World Headquarters:

Fusionary Media
820 Monroe NW, Suite 212
Grand Rapids, MI 49503

Panel 3

the BOX

BENEFITS

Why you should own **the Box**

THE EXHIBIT
FEATURES
BENEFITS
SPEC YOUR OWN
THE DEALER
BUY THE BOX

"Dost thou love life? Then do not squander [the box], for that is the stuff life is made of."

Benjamin Franklin

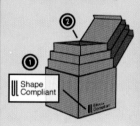

Organization

Compatibility

Image

UL Shape Compliant

1. UL Listed: Shape compliant.
2. Open standard: Compatible with boxes from other manufacturers.

Panel 4

the BOX

BUY THE BOX

Become a proud owner of the **Box**

THE EXHIBIT
FEATURES
BENEFITS
SPEC YOUR OWN
THE DEALER
BUY THE BOX

"There are only two truly infinite things, the universe and [the box]. And I am unsure about the universe."

Albert Einstein

The Box

The Free Gift

Order Form

1. Our classic: the medium, box brown, flap top box.
2. Available for the unbelievable price of $19.95.
3. A free gift with every purchase.

Panel 5

the BOX

THE DEALER

Your exclusive source for **the Box**

THE EXHIBIT
FEATURES
BENEFITS
SPEC YOUR OWN
THE DEALER
BUY THE BOX

he measure of a man what he does with he box]."

Pittacus

About the Dealer

Dealer Location

Contact the Dealer

1. The board room - where we strategize and concept our ideas.
2. The workshop - where we test and modify new technologies.
3. The lab - where creativity reigns supreme.

Panel 6

the BOX

BUY THE BOX

Become a proud owner of the **Box**

THE EXHIBIT
FEATURES
BENEFITS
SPEC YOUR OWN
THE DEALER
BUY THE BOX

"There are only two truly infinite things, the universe and [the box]. And I am unsure about the universe."

Albert Einstein

◄ FRONT

BACK ►

Colors

The Box

The Free Gift

Order Form

1. Easy access holes for neck and arms.
2. Pseudo quote courtesy of Albert Einstein.
3. Roomy fit, short-sleeved, 100% cotton, Beefy-T.

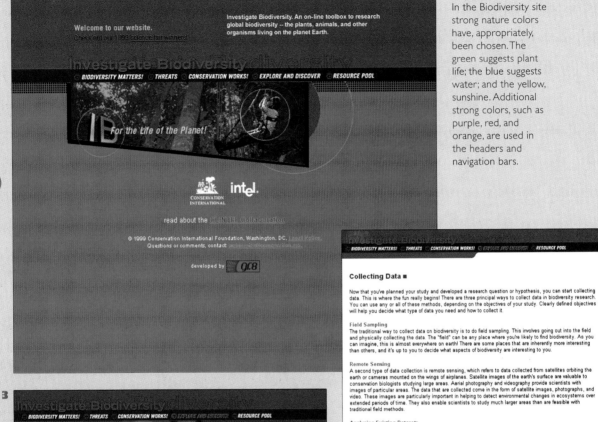

1 | 2 | 3

In the Biodiversity site strong nature colors have, appropriately, been chosen. The green suggests plant life; the blue suggests water; and the yellow, sunshine. Additional strong colors, such as purple, red, and orange, are used in the headers and navigation bars.

Collecting Data ■

Now that you've planned your study and developed a research question or hypothesis, you can start collecting data. This is where the fun really begins! There are three principal ways to collect data in biodiversity research. You can use any or all of these methods, depending on the objectives of your study. Clearly defined objectives will help you decide what type of data you need and how to collect it.

Field Sampling
The traditional way to collect data on biodiversity is to do field sampling. This involves going out into the field and physically collecting the data. The "field" can be any place where you're likely to find biodiversity. As you can imagine, this is almost everywhere on earth! There are some places that are inherently more interesting than others, and it's up to you to decide what aspects of biodiversity are interesting to you.

Remote Sensing
A second type of data collection is remote sensing, which refers to data collected from satellites orbiting the earth or cameras mounted on the wings of airplanes. Satellite images of the earth's surface are valuable to conservation biologists studying large areas. Aerial photography and videography provide scientists with images of particular areas. The data that are collected come in the form of satellite images, photographs, and video. These images are particularly important in helping to detect environmental changes in ecosystems over extended periods of time. They also enable scientists to study much larger areas than are feasible with traditional field methods.

Analyzing Existing Datasets
A third option is to gather data that other people have collected (with their permission, of course) and analyze it in a different way. This is a very good option if you are interested in a part of the world that you can't get to yourself, or if you want to compare the data that you collect with data from other parts of the world. Using existing data sets can be just as challenging as collecting and analyzing your own data.

Biodiversity Matters I Threats I Conservation Works I Explore and Discover I Resource Pool I Home

© 1999 Conservation International Foundation, Washington, DC. Legal Notice.

www.clients.gr8.com

4 | 5 | 6

In the Sylvan School site, conservative dark and royal blues suggest tradition and stability, while the gold is the gilt of achievement.

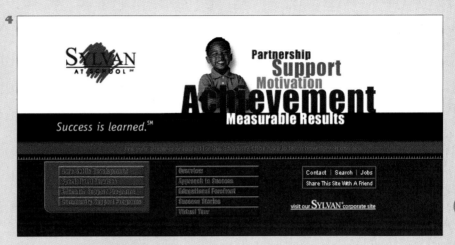

ww.sylvanatschool.com

Overview

Working with you to make a difference.

Over six years ago, Sylvan was challenged by the educational community to provide low-income families and students access to the same tutorial services offered through our learning centers. Accepting this challenge, we initiated our first partnership in 1993 with five of the lowest-performing schools in Baltimore City. Since then, the *Sylvan at School*^SM program has grown to support the individual needs of public and non-public schools, districts and communities across the country to help students realize their full potential.

Today, *Sylvan at School*^SM offers a broad range of services - far beyond its initial focus on core skills: reading and math. We've become an educational resource for school districts. Through school partnerships, we have developed customized, comprehensive solutions that have improved student academic performance, teacher training and parental involvement in nearly 900 schools across 130 school districts nationwide. And what's more...we guarantee results.

In addition, *Sylvan at School*^SM has carefully acquired the expertise to assist school districts with the

1 | 2 | 3 | 4 | 5 | 6

These three sites demonstrate how pastels and curved shapes on a white background can create a subtle effect. Aptly, for the Photographers site (*1, 2, 3*) the conceit is to use icons from conventional print for authentication purposes. Registration marks, tint and color bars, and typographical construction lines have all been used for adornment. The look of a grid sheet on the opening screen takes this a stage further. The Meteorit site (*6*) is high-key, elegant, and multilayered, and equally garnished with

www.photographers.de

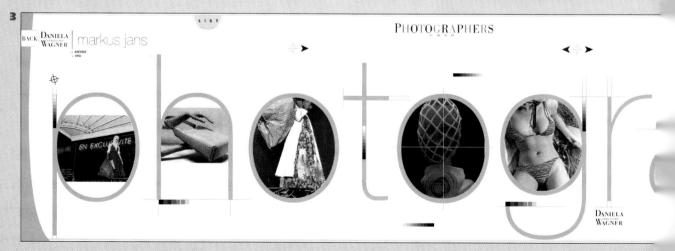

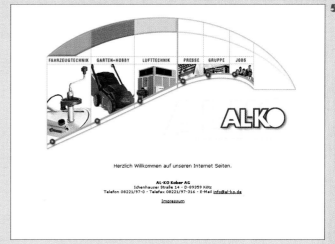

www.al-ko.com

6

construction lines. Alko (4, 5) is in the unglamorous business of making trailer hitches and chassis, with lawnmower manufacture for light relief. The firm has chosen white for the ground with red for emphasis.

www.coma2.com

www.maxwelllive.com

www.jenniferlopez.com

www.jewel-web.com

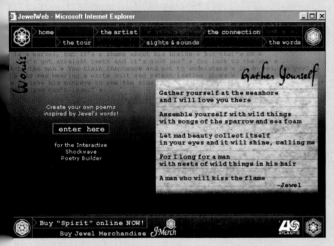

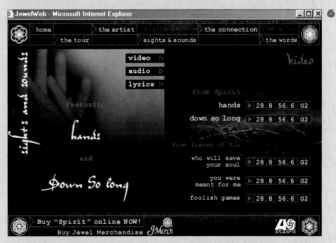

1 | 2 | 3 | 4 | 5 | 6 | 7

hese screens all
emonstrate the use
f the duotone
mage. The Maxwell
te (1) features
nderwater graphics
nd the turquoise
olors of tropical
aters, but nobody
oks good in that
ade of green. The
nnifer Lopez site
,3), on the other
nd, shows off the
onomy of style that
cord-sleeve

designers are expert
at. The site designers
have placed a visual
pun on the screens:
Web design is a
rectangular activity,
and self-referential
construction lines
have been left onsite.
The well-judged reds
and browns are
complemented by
the pale blue. The
Jewel site (4, 5, 6, 7)
offers a variety of
duotone mood

shades alongside
busy design and an
imaginative script
typeface to add
atmosphere.

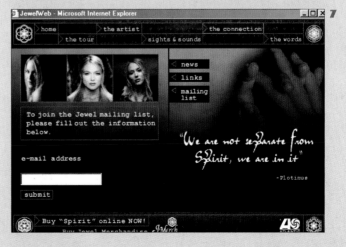

122

www.ldg.be

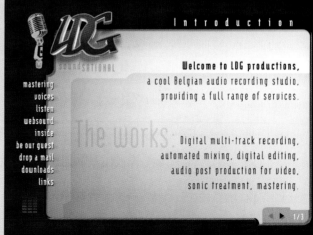

1 | 2 | 3

The unifying theme of the sites on this spread is the motion picture. In their different ways, each is concerned with evoking the movies or going to the movies.

The LDG site uses three reds to create a plush effect, recalling the red velvet drapes and old-fashioned seats. This movie-going theme hangs together with the

silvery gray of the wide text area—the red velvet curtains having opened to reveal the "silver screen".

www.hollywoodpartners.de

Hollywood Partners Medien AG
Maximilianstrasse 30 - D-80539 München, Germany
Telefon: +49 (0)89 / 24 20 62 - 0
Telefax: +49 (0)89 / 24 20 62 - 20
E-Mail: info@hollywoodpartners.de

Bitte benutzen Sie für unsere Website mindest. einen 4.0 Browser

Website Design und Produktion von coma2 - collective of media artists

Letztes Update am 11. Februar 2000

Jetzt:
Der neue TV-Spot
zum Anschauen und Herunterladen.

MOVIES

PASSION

Story:
Eine Leidenschaft für Musik, fürs Leben und für eine bestimmte Form sexueller Lust, die vor der Öffentlichkeit geheim gehalten werden muß – das sind die Themen, um die es in diesem aufsehenerregenden und provokativen Film geht. Richard Roxburgh spielt den passionierten Komponisten und Pianisten Percy Grainger; Barbara Hershey gibt eine unvergeßliche Darstellung als seine eifersüchtige Mutter, Emily Woof spielt die strahlend schöne Musikstudentin, die es wagt sich zwischen die beiden zu drängen und ihr perverses Geheimnis zu ergründen.

Regie:
Peter Duncan machte 1995 seinen vielgelobten Debutfilm "Children of The Revolution", der drei "Australian Film Institute

www.hitchcock100.com

4 | 5 | 6 | 7

Hollywood Partners (4, 5) love movies, and the more cinematic the movie, the more they love it. In the swooping three-color drive-by home page there are small-screen tricks to savor: the translucent film reels, type distortion which follows the curves of the page, and an unusual attention to detail in the stylish edge finish around the top of the page. Universal Studios (6, 7) celebrates the centenary of Alfred Hitchcock's birth in high-contrast horror style. The correctly adjusted monitor will show monochrome—try turning up the green for a satisfyingly ghoulish effect.

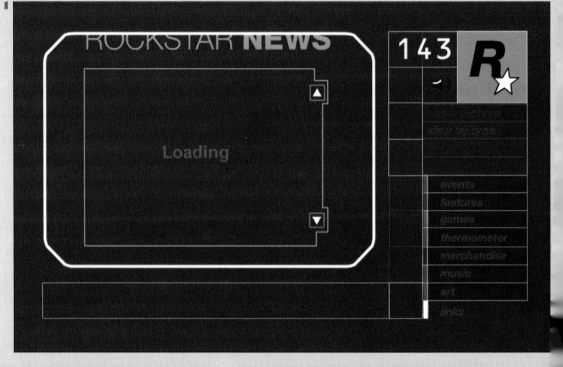

www.rockstargames.com

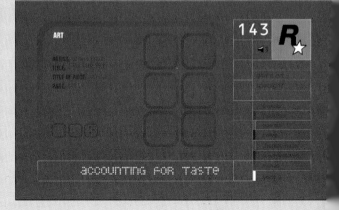

1 | 2 | 3 | 4 | 5 | 6 | 7

These screens all show the use of strong, bright background colors with limited text and image in the foreground. They grab attention with their simplicity and boldness. Rockstar News (*1, 2, 3*) is unafraid to use neon green, although the brightness of the background is mitigated to some extent by a darker, more moderate green. Flat color and Flash drive Formitas, a Slovenian marketing and PR site (*5, 6, 7*). After the moiré wheel has done its turn, skill is required to chase and click on your chosen topic as it rotates at a brisk pace; more well-selected colors follow, giving the site a classy modern look. The Züritel site (*4*) follows the same basic principle, though a contrasting blue has been added to the rich orange ground to pick out the company's name.

Feedback   Kontakt   Suche   Sitemap

ZÜRITEL

Z ZÜRICH KOSMOS direkt

Autoversichern

Produktinfos

Prämienangebot

Onlineabwicklung

Kundencenter

Game   Winner

4

125

Neu: Berechnen Sie **on**line Ihre Prämie   Hier klicken!

www.zuritel.ch

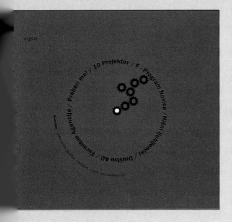

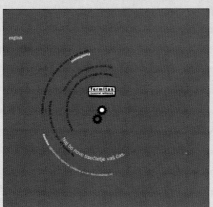

6

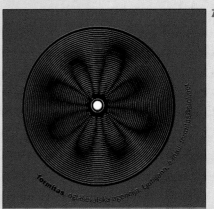

7

www.formitas.si

www.rullkoetter.de

1 | 2 | 3 | 4 | 5 | 6

The look of both these sites is somber; though unrelated, they have strong design similarities which have their roots in print. An enthusiasm for calligraphic type forms is evident, but it's the expert management of small graduations of black that distinguishes these sites from the usual crowd.

4

Impressum

Produziert von

DER POOL - Team für Werbung, Rothenbaumchaussee 193-195, 20149 Hamburg
Telefon (o 40) 41 46 47-0, Telefax (o 40) 44 43 22, e-mail: info@der-pool.de

Konzept, Design & Umsetzung

Dirk Rullkötter AGD (Werbung + Design), Kleines Heenfeld 19, 32278 Kirchlengern
Telefon (o 52 23) 7 34 90, Telefax (o 52 23) 76 02 30, e-mail: info@rullkoetter.iok.net
http://www.rullkoetter.iok.net

Audio-Postproduction („Eulentraum" © toi, toi, toi Records 1998)
Studio Funk KG Hamburg (Berlin, Düsseldorf, Frankfurt am Main),
ussee 69, 20259 Hamburg,
32 04-3, Telefax (o 40) 4 32 04-500, e-mail: info@studiofunk.de

Die Aktion
Schirmherrschaft
Das Gemälde
Jugendwerk
Förderkreis
Glasaktie
Der Künstler

127

Der Künstler

Die Aktion
Schirmherrschaft
Das Gemälde
Jugendwerk
Förderkreis
Glasaktie
Der Künstler

Impressum

ww.schatten.de

6

Die Aktion
Schirmherrschaft
Das Gemälde
Jugendwerk
Förderkreis
Glasaktie
Der Künstler

Impressum

Eine Aktion des „Förderkreis zugunsten Jugendwerk"

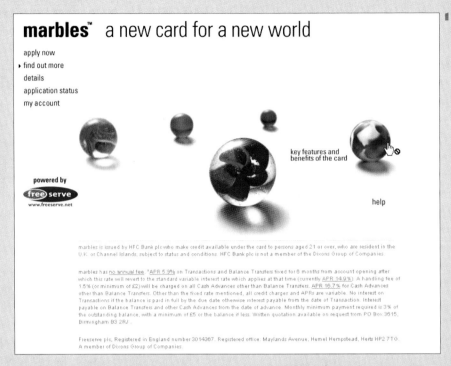

www.fscard.co.uk

www.kompan.co

1 | 2 | 3

Marbles (*1*) is a charge card company. Its look represents a welcome change in the methods of the brand development industry—from the designer's perspective at least. In a market now terribly short of words to imply success, financial probity, and status, the trend is toward visual whimsy. Hundreds of such cards offer the same or similar; maybe the cheery aspect and playground memory of marbles is enough to distinguish one from the crowd. In the world of real children, playground equipment makers Kompan (*2, 3*) make do with a rubber fish.

4

www.woodblock.simplenet.com

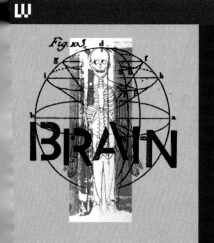

6

More to come, just give me some
time to breath first, ok?

98 [Kariyanet](#)

[Rollin' Ice](#)

97 [Tibetan Freedom](#)

Velvet - [Blur](#)

Velvet - [Brian Wilson](#)

Velvet - [Cactus Child](#)

Velvet - [Cordrazine](#)

Velvet - [Homepage](#)

Velvet - [Jimi Hendrix](#)

Velvet - [Skunkhour](#)

Velvet - [Snuff](#)

96 Channel X - [Cult TV](#)

Channel X - [Fryday](#)

[Digital Alchemist](#)

| 5 | 6
San Francisco, Kha
oang professes
nself to be a
ughty child with
oetulant opening
essage and climbing-
me graphics.

www.movedesign.com

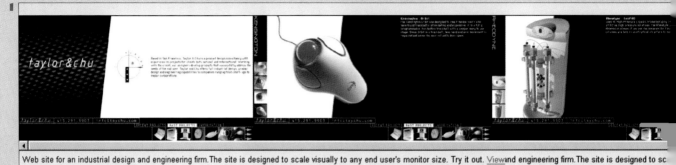

Web site for an industrial design and engineering firm. The site is designed to scale visually to any end user's monitor size. Try it out. View and engineering firm. The site is designed to sc

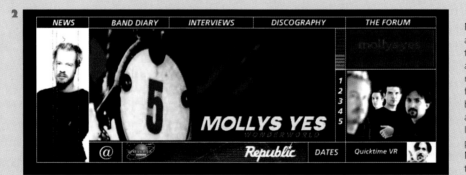

www.mollysyes.com

1 | 2 | 3

Move Design (*1*) offers an interesting angle on the problem of scaling any viewer's monitor resolution. Visit the site for a demonstration but be prepared for an immediate and lengthy Shockwave player download. Mollys Yes (*2, 3*) follows the simpler rock band tradition of mailbox-shaped windows. Move Design is fond of its blue trackball; the band has an affection for the green sound level meter.

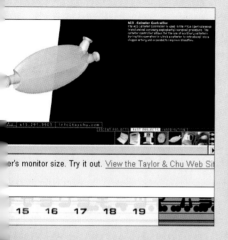

er's monitor size. Try it out. <u>View the Taylor & Chu Web Site</u>

15 16 17 18 19

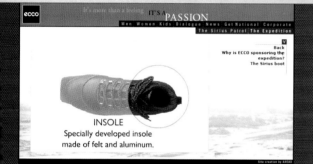

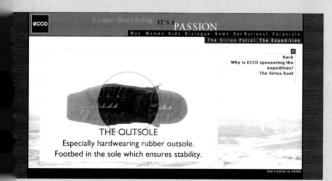

www.ecco.com

4 | 5 | 6 | 7

Those suffering from bad feet can luxuriate in the soothing balm of the Ecco shoes site while aspiring to own such costly but life-enhancing footwear. Layers of pastel blue in the background image are picked up in the navigation bars and make an effective foil for the red link buttons.

1

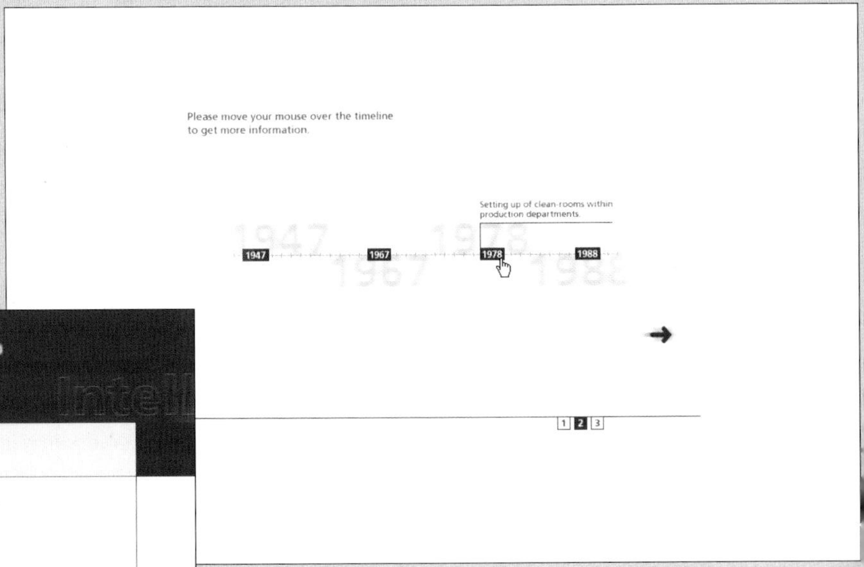

Please move your mouse over the timeline
to get more information.

Setting up of clean-rooms within
production departments.

1947   1967   1978   1988

1 2 3

2

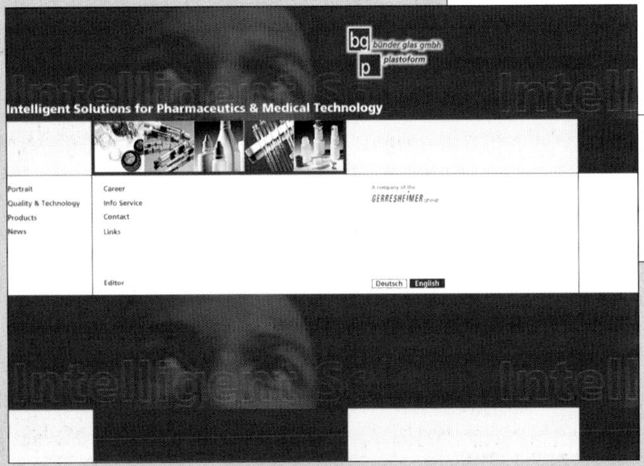

bg bünder glas gmbh
p plastoform

Intelligent Solutions for Pharmaceutics & Medical Technology

Portrait   Career
Quality & Technology   Info Service   A company of the
Products   Contact   *GERRESHEIMER group*
News   Links

Editor   Deutsch | English

www.buenderglas.com

www.wyland.com

3

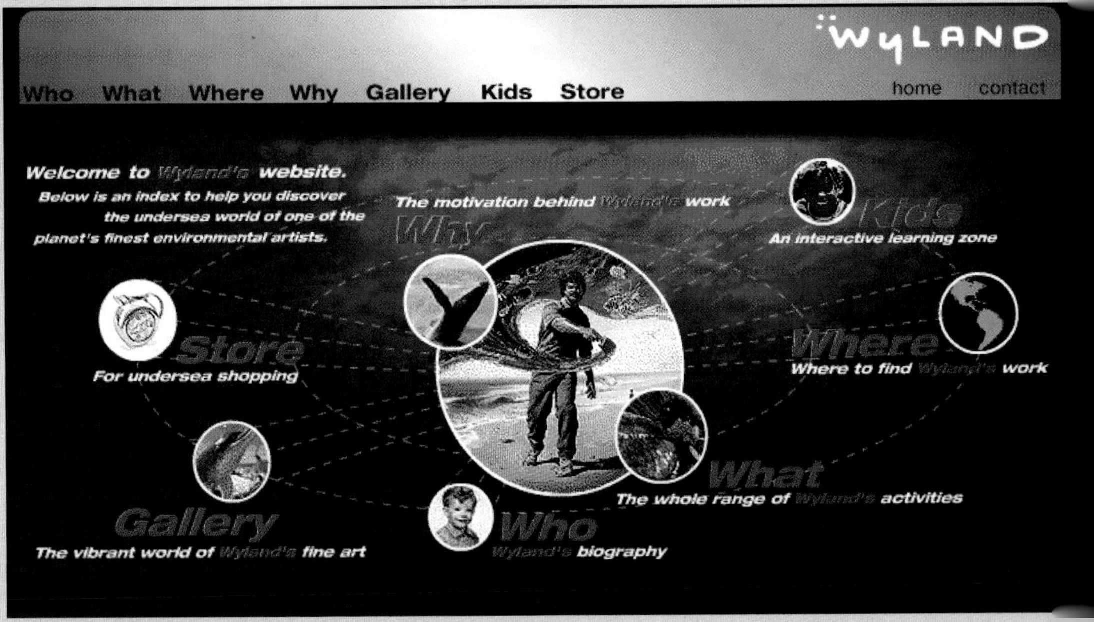

WYLAND

Who   What   Where   Why   Gallery   Kids   Store   home   contact

Welcome to *Wyland's* website.
Below is an index to help you discover
the undersea world of one of the
planet's finest environmental artists.

The motivation behind *Wyland's* work

Why

Kids
An interactive learning zone

Store
For undersea shopping

Where
Where to find *Wyland's* work

What
The whole range of *Wyland's* activities

Gallery
The vibrant world of *Wyland's* fine art

Who
Wyland's biography

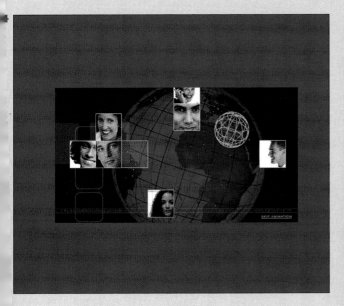

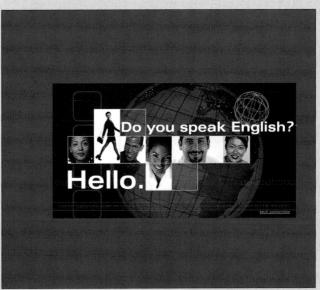

1 | 2 | 3 | 4 | 5 | 6 | 7

Günder Glas (*1, 2*) uses blue with a lighter version of the same blue in a duotone-photo effect. The same lighter blue in shadow lettering adds an extra layer of texture. The slogan and corporate logo are in reversed-out white lettering, while the main text area has a white ground with blue lettering. A small amount of yellow appears in the icons. The Wyland site (*3*) shows the same basic color structure, but uses three blues with a contrasting yellow to highlight. Reversed-out white lettering is also used on the Wall Street Institute site (*4, 5, 6, 7*). British readers will not be surprised to see the English language promoted in red, white, and blue, but it is clear from the logo and style that this is the US version.

www.wallstreetinstitute.com

1

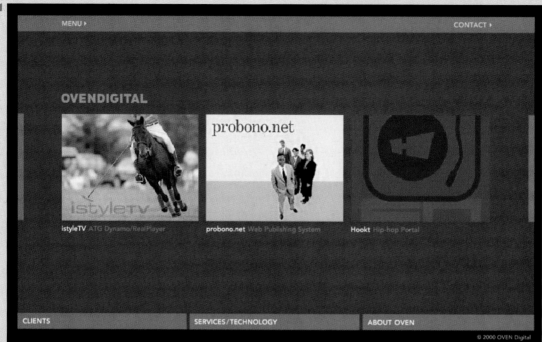

1 | 2 | 3 | 4 | 5
International outfit Oven Digital (1, 2, 3) opts for a color solution that emphasizes the firm's portfolio shots, while their own corporate image recedes into the background. Gray screens are garnished with yellow prompts throughout with GIF type (no HTML anywhere) in only gray, black, or white. German advertising agency Wiesmeier (4, 5) is even more recessive, with light cream and pale gray in profusion. Even the background piano music is hyper-discreet. A little color is allowed on a subsequent screen (5), and even a punning reference to hard/heart selling.

2

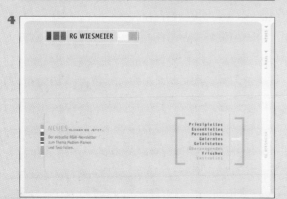

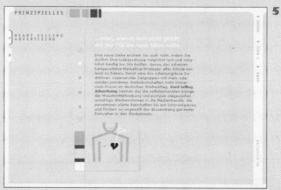

3 www.ovendigital.co

4

5

www.wiesmeier.de

6 | 7 | 8

Pos IT is a market leader in Web design in Tasmania, and the company's site shows that although design on the Web knows no boundaries, there are variations which must be due to local experience. Who *is* that guy?

http://www.posit.com.au

6

135

Sun Netra Range
DTS
Ascend
Cisco
Aironet
Netscape

sIT have reseller arrangements with
ese companies and also use and
ommend their products.

products

communications

positive

www.posit.com.au

about us
clients
products
services
contact
home

information technology

positive

8

Posit have been acknowledged by
ese clients as their preferred Internet
and New Media production house.

clients

positive

information technology

www.simplymodern.com

1 | 2 | 3 | 4 | 5

Purveyors of right-brain style with left-brain sensibility, Simply Modern uses Web-safe yellow-green (CCCC00) and brown (660000) for emphasis throughout its site (1, 2). This may not seem like much harmony but the disturbing addition of the fire announcement, set in red, shows that the underlying scheme works very well. The same green recurs in the e-media-c site (3, 4, 5), but allied with a toning and Web-safe darker shade (999900). In this case, however, the introduction of a strong purple tends to tip the balance.

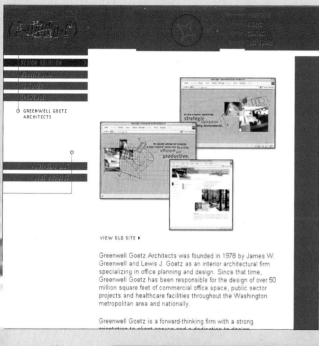

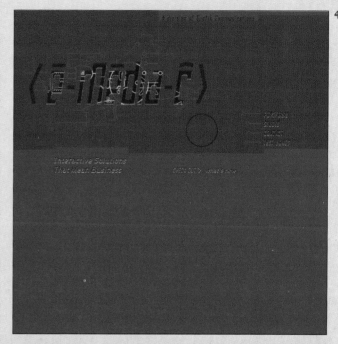

VIEW OLD SITE ▶

Greenwell Goetz Architects was founded in 1978 by James W. Greenwell and Lewis J. Goetz as an interior architectural firm specializing in office planning and design. Since that time, Greenwell Goetz has been responsible for the design of over 50 million square feet of commercial office space, public sector projects and healthcare facilities throughout the Washington metropolitan area and nationally.

Greenwell Goetz is a forward-thinking firm with a strong orientation to client service and a dedication to design.

137

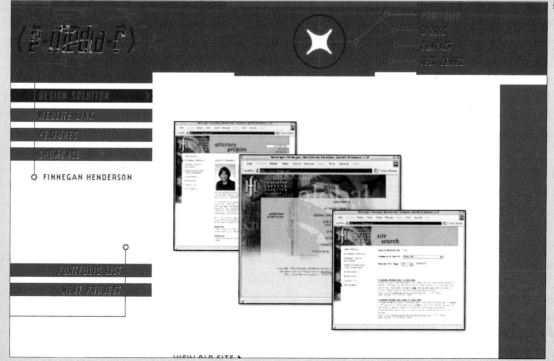

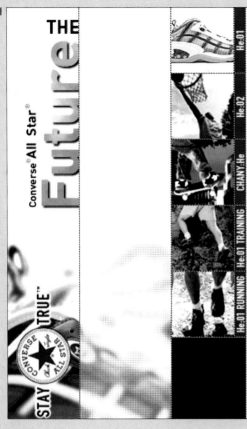

The He:01 is just the beginning. We're planning an entire line that will include shoes for cross-training, traditional running, and trail running, as well as a second basketball shoe. Learn more from the images on the left.

HELIUM TECHNOLOGY

THE COMMERCIAL

PRODUCT LINE

ENDORSERS

RETAILERS

CONVERSE NEWS

CONTACT CONVERSE

www.converse.com

1 | 2 | 3
They're putting helium in your shoes now! The sports shoes manufacturers were very early on the Web, and Converse (1) shows that the logo is all, reserving the only contrasting color for its exclusive use in a sea of white. Solid German investment bankers, Templeton (2, 3), are white as the driven snow as well, with their portfolio manager rendered in a trustworthy blue duotone.

www.templeton.de

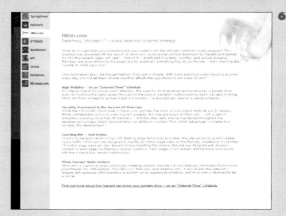

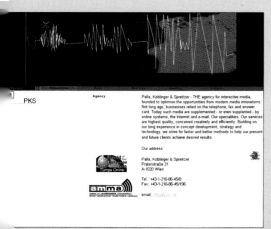

4 | 5 | 6 | 7 | 8
Equal amounts of white, but with discreet doses of hot color for emphasis, characterize the markedly similar sites of e-business firms Sapient (4, 5, 6) of the US and PKS (7, 8) in Vienna, though the latter allows itself a zany and mysterious introductory artwork.

139

www.sapient.com

www.pks.at

1 | 2 | 3

Once upon a time, there was a visionary, possibly a printer, who invented the tabbed index card. One day his descendants will arrive in town to demand their long overdue royalty payments for the countless billions of occasions upon which the motif has been used on screen. When they come, you'll recognize them easily from their radiused corners and fetching highlights. Still, the tab works, and these two sites confirm that it is a powerful device, especially when allied with strong and contrasting color.

www.informative.com

www.ishop.com

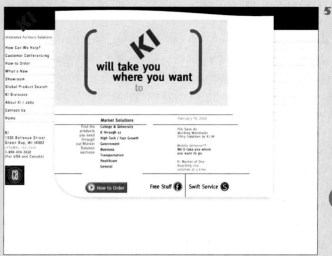

www.ki-inc.com

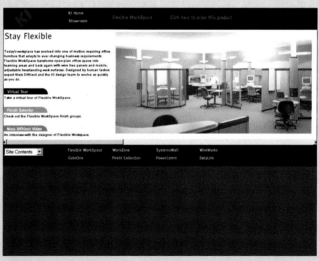

www.astd.org

4 | 5 | 6 | 7

KI Furniture (4, 5, 6) are tabless and bold on their homepage, but they know curved corners too! And the shadows that go with them. Back in the mainstream, the trainers' virtual community site ASTD (7) struggles in the frame's straitjacket.

www.blackbean.com

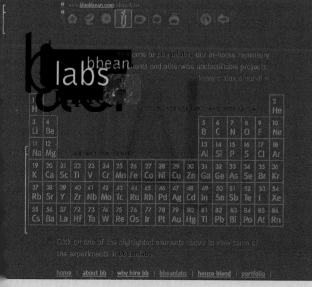

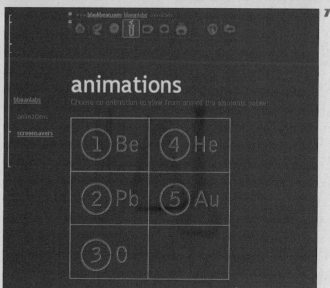

|2|3|4|5|6|7

tting the "poop"
Boston's Black
an studio is a
omatic sensation
rth experiencing.
e hoary old
buchet MS

typeface is given a
comprehensive
workout in the
background, but
survives in stinging
color as the screens
unfold.

OOTWORLD RELEASE:/ #3

VISUAL DESIGNER MIRCO PASQUALINI VIRTUAL LAB

SELECT:/IMAGE

GALLERY:

INFORMATION

This is my collection (again under building) of my typographics works make for a personal exibition.

All of this picture are large of 50x70 cm and printed in a lucid special support, water resisten. If ou are interested buy someone, write to me mircox@seven.it

1 | 2 | 3 | 4 | 5 | 6

Mirco Pasqualini is the enthusiastic creator of Ootworld (*1, 2, 3*), an ambitious outpost of Flash-based typographic and color fun. Equally otherworldly, Heavy.com (*4, 5, 6*) offers equally ambitious music tracks served over a bed of Japanese comic art. Both sites can crash your browser.

OOTWORLD RELEASE./ #3

VISUAL DESIGNER MIRCO PASQUALINI VIRTUAL LAB

ABOUT ME: PERSONAL INFORMATION

NAME: MIRCO
SURNAME: PASQUALINI
EMAIL: MIRCOX@SEVEN.IT
WEBSITE: HTTP://WWW.OOTWORLD.COM
BORN: 7 DECEMBER 1978

PRESS: INTERVIEW ONLINE AND MAGAZINE

www.ootworld.com

OOTWORLD RELEASE./ #3

VISUAL DESIGNER MIRCO PASQUALINI VIRTUAL LAB

/IMAGE #14

GALLERY:
INFORMATION

ww.heavy.com

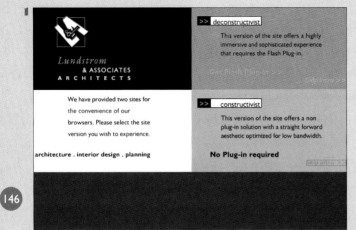

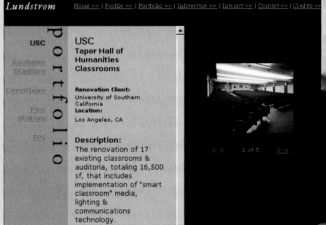

www.lundstrom.com

1 | 2 | 3 | 4 | 5 | 6 | 7 | 8 | 9

Two sites which suggest the beginning of a tradition and its simultaneous ending. Architects on the Web have adopted the colors of stone, earth, sand, and grass as their stock-in-trade (1, 2, 3, 4). And they like to build with type. So it is a not unwelcome surprise to find the Ford Mustang heritage site successfully stealing the architects' clothes (5, 6, 7, 8, 9).

5

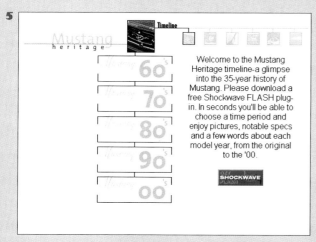

Welcome to the Mustang Heritage timeline-a glimpse into the 35-year history of Mustang. Please download a free Shockwave FLASH plug-in. In seconds you'll be able to choose a time period and enjoy pictures, notable specs and a few words about each model year, from the original to the '00.

6

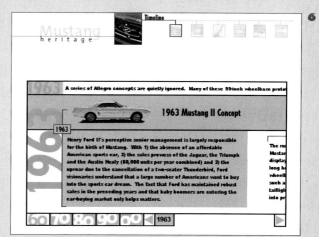

147

7

8

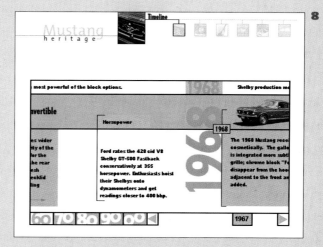

9

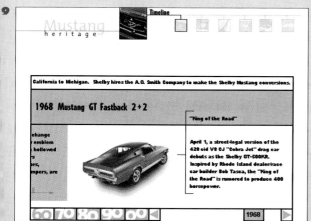

www.fordheritage.com

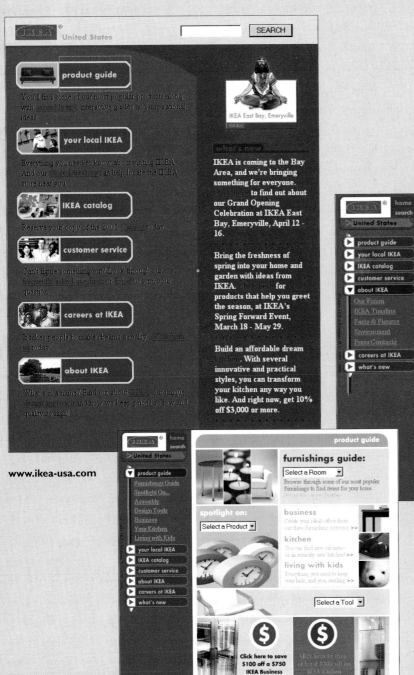

148

www.ikea-usa.com

1 | 2 | 3 | 4 | 5 | 6 | 7

Yellow is optimistic and sunny (qualities absolutely essential in the prospective constructor of assembly-required furniture). IKEA runs the entire color gamut, from the expected cool home page through to an incendiary red "living with children" screen equipped with green text links. Relax with the IVAR do-it-yourself closet-building option before attempting the real thing.

Playing is a child's way of understanding the world. Each new experience builds on the past and creates learning. So we designed children's furniture and toys that are ..., creating, pretending and, most importantly, having fun!

Living with children means being prepared for their different stages. One year they might want to be an astronaut, the next a veterinarian. And they need furnishings that adapt easily to their different changes. Luckily, our affordable line of children's products are ready for your child's wild imagination...and their wild adventures!

MAMMUT wardrobe holds clothes, toys and everything else they'll need for their first trip to the moon.

Need More Space?

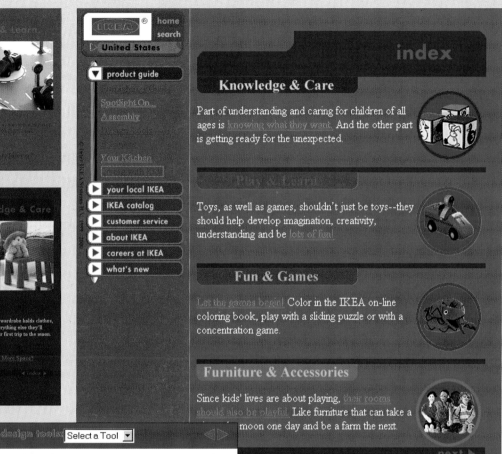

index

Knowledge & Care

Part of understanding and caring for children of all ages is knowing what they want. And the other part is getting ready for the unexpected.

Play & Learn

Toys, as well as games, shouldn't just be toys--they should help develop imagination, creativity, understanding and be lots of fun!

Fun & Games

Let the games begin! Color in the IKEA on-line coloring book, play with a sliding puzzle or with a concentration game.

Furniture & Accessories

Since kids' lives are about playing, their rooms should also be playful. Like furniture that can take a ... moon one day and be a farm the next.

next ▶

design tools: Select a Tool ▼

POÄNG Design Tool

Looking for the perfect chair? With our POÄNG design tool you can create one that's perfect for you. You can find the right cushion, color and frame for your style.

Brighter Living

Don't just light your home. Learn how to decorate with light with the IKEA Guide to Brighter Living. You'll find everything you need to know about lighting -- for every room in your home.

IVAR Design Tool

With our easy-to-use IVAR design tool you can create a custom IVAR storage system to fit into any space in your home. Whatever your storage needs may be, it will help you make the most out of your living area.

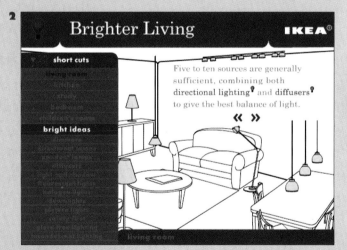

150

www.ikea-usa.com

1│2│3│4│5│6│7│8│9│10

The IKEA site grows organically, with differing design styles to address distinct topics. This is in direct contrast to the company's printed catalog output, where uniformity of approach is the rule. The lighting section, for example (*1,2,3, 4*), here takes off on a new color scheme and monochrome drawing style. So far so good with those shelves. . .

5

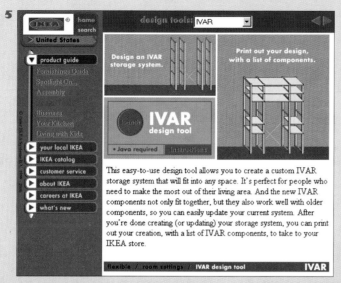

This easy-to-use design tool allows you to create a custom IVAR storage system that will fit into any space. It's perfect for people who need to make the most out of their living area. And the new IVAR components not only fit together, but they also work well with older components, so you can easily update your current system. After you're done creating (or updating) your storage system, you can print out your creation, with a list of IVAR components, to take to your IKEA store.

6

151

8

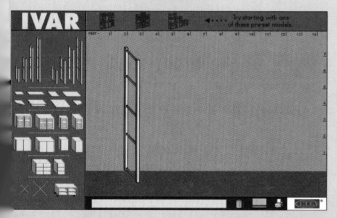

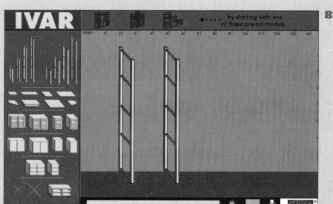

10

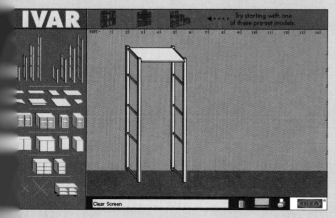

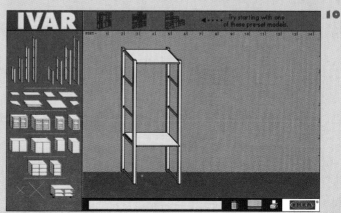

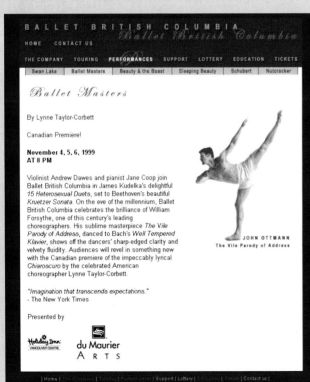

1 | 2
Rich chocolate-box
colors with a light
touch of gilt dignify
the Ballet British
Columbia site. Cream
centers for the text
panels and a nicely
judged cream
duotone complete
the picture.

www.lacountyarts.org

www.balletbc.com

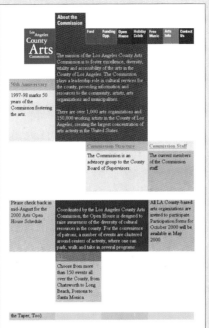

3 |4 |5 |6 |7 |8

In Los Angeles, the gridlock extends to the city's cultural life. Once accustomed to the layout, however, you'll find the blocks begin to make sense, and the harmonizing colors are a useful unifying device. Charles de Gaulle famously complained that France would never be unified except by fear, since it had 265 different kinds of cheese; Los Angeles County has 5,000 working artists.

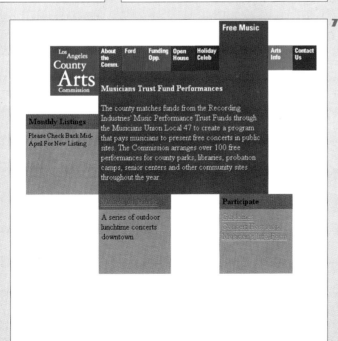

154

www.ideo.com

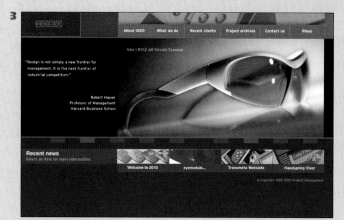

1 | 2 | 3 | 4 | 5 | 6 | 7 | 8 | 9

Industrial designers Ideo take an unconventional line to display their wares. Trusting in the viewer's enthusiasm for horizontal scrolling, the opening blueprint screen offers a grand total of 70 different project studies. The blue ground device continues into each project screen, including that for the new Transmeta Webslate (*1*), which will ultimately sound the death-knell for panoramic presentations like these.

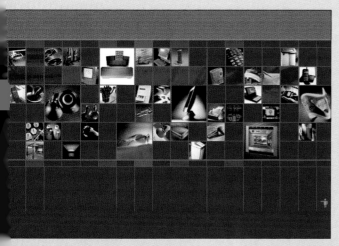

2

Transmeta | Webslate Concept

IDEO's conceptual design for a modular computer showcases the abilities of the new Crusoe microprocessor from Transmeta. Transmeta commissioned IDEO to design a portable, modular "webslate" concept to demonstrate potential products enabled by their new software-based chip technology. The webslate incorporates a high-resolution, eight-inch touchscreen for viewing web pages, DVD movies, and more. The webslate offers greater portability and more discreet use than a laptop, and offers a larger, more robust viewing area compared to today's handheld PDAs.

IDEO's concept has at its center a slim, two-layer slate which accommodates plug-in modules for various applications. The modules can be added to any of the four sides for landscape or portrait format, and include a camera for on-the-road videoconferencing, a GPS module for navigation, audio speakers and controls for downloaded music, and modules for game playing across the web. A snap-on cover protects the screen and provides a folding

155

6

Amtrak | Acela

Amtrak engaged IDEO to propose a strategy for its new high-speed rail service between Boston and Washington, D.C. The challenge was to differentiate rail travel from airlines and automobiles in quality of service across all aspects of the experience of rail travel. IDEO identified ten steps in the passenger's journey, from learning about Amtrak and planning a trip through to arriving at the destination and continuing on.

To understand Amtrak's vision, IDEO's team rode trains, toured stations, interviewed senior management, and analyzed Amtrak's information distribution and advertising campaigns. They conducted in-depth user profiles and studied Amtrak's customer research. This

BBC | Digital Radios

IDEO designed these radio concepts to exploit the advantages of the BBC's new digital broadcast services. IDEO brainstorming generated design ideas which were built into user scenarios to explore the appearance and operation of the radios. Displays on the radios show pictorial information to complement the audio program, such as musician portraits, sports factoids, program guides or recording set-up information. Designs range from home radios that can be instantly personalized by family members to personal portable radios and radios for the shower.

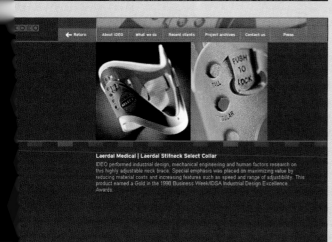

9

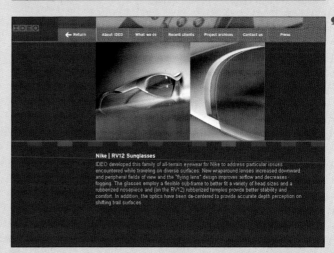

Laerdal Medical | Laerdal Stifneck Select Collar

IDEO performed industrial design, mechanical engineering and human factors research on this highly adjustable neck brace. Special emphasis was placed on maximizing value by reducing material costs and increasing features such as speed and range of adjustibility. This product earned a Gold in the 1998 Business Week/IDSA Industrial Design Excellence Awards.

Nike | RV12 Sunglasses

IDEO developed this family of all-terrain eyewear for Nike to address particular issues encountered while traveling on diverse surfaces: New wraparound lenses increased downward and peripheral fields of view and the "flying lens" design improves airflow and decreases fogging. The glasses employ a flexible sub-frame to better fit a variety of head sizes and a rubberized nosepiece and (on the RV12) rubberized temples provide better stability and comfort. In addition, the optics have been de-centered to provide accurate depth perception on shifting trail surfaces.

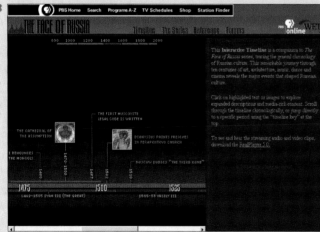

www.pbs.org

1 | 2 | 3 | 4

The "Face of Russia" site uses opulent reds and golds to suggest both Russia's imperial history and its more recent communist past. Extensive vertical and horizontal color graduations make the site a challenge for low-grade browsers, but the strong overall color design keeps it all together.

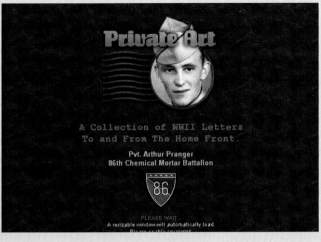

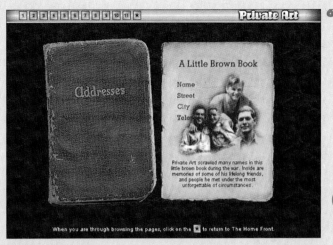

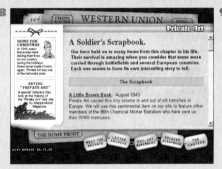

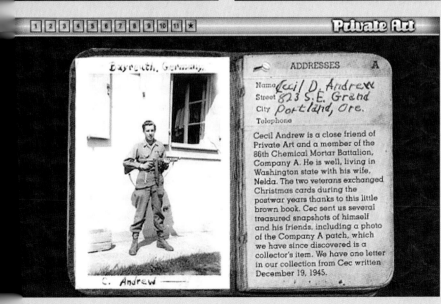

5 | 6 | 7 | 8 | 9 | 10

The Private Art(hur Pranger) site is a careful tribute to a lost world, dressed in the colors of faded fatigues. It is curious that our perception of this era makes this site look authentic; the small amount of "natural color" film shot at the time, though rarely known, is shocking in its bright intensity.

www.private-art.com

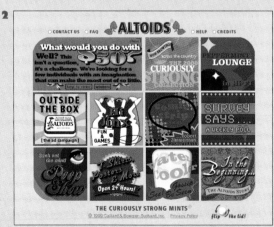

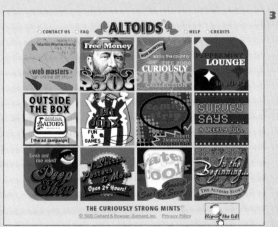

www.altoids.com

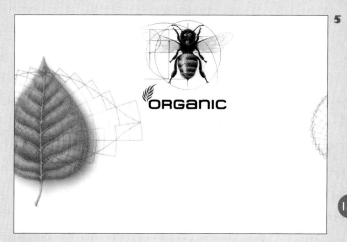

5

159

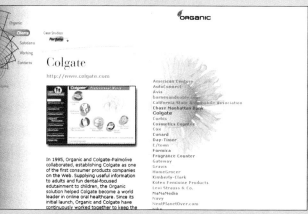

7

8

|2|3|4|5|6|7|8

hese two sites, ough their fields of peration could ardly be more fferent, show the eb at what it does st—illusion and ssociation. Altoids nts are 12mm (half inch) in diameter d taste strongly of ppermint, but not re strongly, to this observer, than similar confectionery. This whimsical site (1, 2, 3), however, manages to invest them with a range of typographic associations which employ devices from every corner of the Web portfolio, all wrapped in a pale fondant background. At first glance, Organic (4, 5, 6, 7, 8) might appear to be selling health food— there are bees and leaves aplenty—but no, it's e-business in another coat. Leonardo's man in a circle would spin in his grave if he knew that the leaves had been designed in FreeHand.

www.organic.com

E-HEALTH & INFORMATION
TECHNOLOGY

MEDICAL TECHNOLOGY

DRUG DISCOVERY
& DEVELOPMENT

HEALTH CARE SERVICES

With over $300 million in committed capital, Delphi's investment interests encompass every segment of the healthcare field, including:

- E-Health & Information Technology
- Medical Technology
- Drug Discovery & Development
- Health Care Services

About Delphi | Our Team | Our Companies | News | Contact Us | Home

Copyright © 2000   Delphi Ventures, 3000 Sand Hill Road, Building 1, Suite 135, Menlo Park, CA 94025 (650) 854-9650

Site designed by Stratford Internet Technologies Inc.

1 | 2 | 3
A rosy glow pervades the Delphi Ventures site. Old pre-press operators would have toiled for hours to lose the magenta cast in the headline transparencies, but we are so familiar with deliberately shifting color balance that they slide by almost unnoticed. Deep blue, it should be noted, is the color of financial probity, and may be renamed Banker's Blue in some future Web specification.

www.delphiventures.com

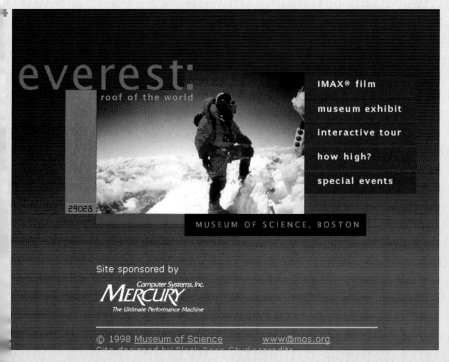

everest:
roof of the world

29028

IMAX® film

museum exhibit

interactive tour

how high?

special events

MUSEUM OF SCIENCE, BOSTON

Site sponsored by
Computer Systems, Inc.
MERCURY
The Ultimate Performance Machine

© 1998 Museum of Science   www@mos.org
Site designed by Black Bean Studios

home   IMAX® film   exhibit   tour   how high?   special events

everest:

in this section:
calendar
trip to Nepal
related links

There are no climbs Everest mostly.

Plan an adventure of your own. Here a more information on trip to Nepal.

Home | IMAX Film | Exhibit | Tour | How High? | Special Events

home   IMAX® film   exhibit   tour   how high?   special events

everest:
the film

EVEREST
MacGillivray-Freeman Films

NOTE: *EVEREST* the film is not currently showing at the Omni Theater.

Mt. Everest towers more than 29,000 feet into the sky. At the summit, the body gets only one-third the oxygen available at sea level. The view is literally breathtaking. Now, the Mugar Omni Theater at the Museum of Science in Boston offers a chance to join a team of world-class

home   IMAX® film   exhibit   tour   how high?   special events

how high
is high?

747 cruising altitude 34,000 ft. (10,362m)

Everest summit 29,028 ft. (8850m)

SOUTH AMERICA
Aconcagua 22,841 ft. (6960m)

NORTH AMERICA

4|5|6|7|8 With the aid of IMAX cinema, you can now virtually stand on the summit of Everest. Boston Museum of Science's Everest site elegantly sets off the hard-won images on rich grounds of saturated color.

www.mos.org

home   IMAX® film   exhibit   tour   how high?   special events

everest:
the exhibit
roof of the world

in this section
plate tectonics
physiological effects
reviews

Complementing the largest film ever shot on Mt. Everest is a one-of-a-kind exhibit that draws on tremendous ties between the Museum of Science and the grandest mountain on earth. Open exclusively in Boston with the film *EVEREST*, the exhibit explores the science and history that enshroud the Himalaya Mountains. This unique exhibit goes further to explain the challenges met by Honorary Director Bradford Washburn and other scientists in two official expeditions on Everest, whose tasks included

1

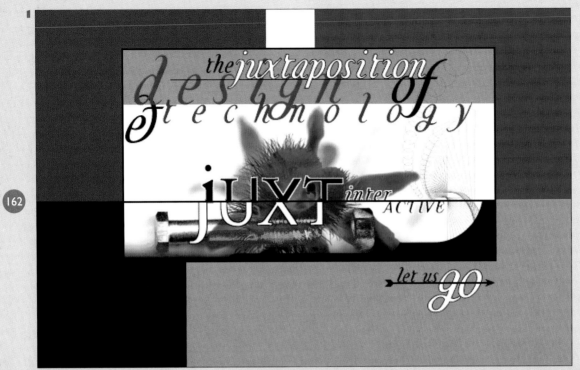

1 | 2 | 3
Juxt Interactive uses Flash to create a highly mannered movie which borrows heavily from the old typography. This simple approach contrasts with the fearsome bazaar of their home page (*1*).

2

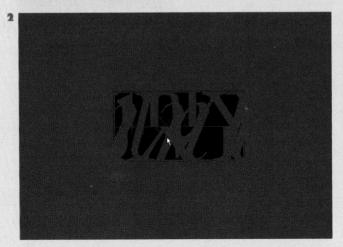

www.juxtinteractive.com

welcome | choose your version   **flash**   **html**   **palm**

www.nexus-group.de

4 | 5 | 6

Flash is to the fore also at Nexus, but in conjunction with a cool European look. Twinkling monochrome panels chase each other around the headline bar; traces of hairline rules distinguish the restrained type design.

1|2
Nike now offers
home movies to
those who are
disinclined to jog to
the movie theater.
And there are other
advantages—you can
view the action in any
order you choose.
The tabbed navigation
bars carry posterized
GIFs, and the bars
themselves cast
shadows on the
background.

www.nike.com

3

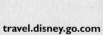

travel.disney.go.com

3 | 4 | 5
Virtuoso frame
design from Disney.
All is light, bright, and
enthusiastic across all
the different sites
under the Disney
umbrella. Toy Story
(5) rates a textured
background, but
otherwise, the
color values and
backgrounds are
utterly familiar.

5

www.disney.co.uk

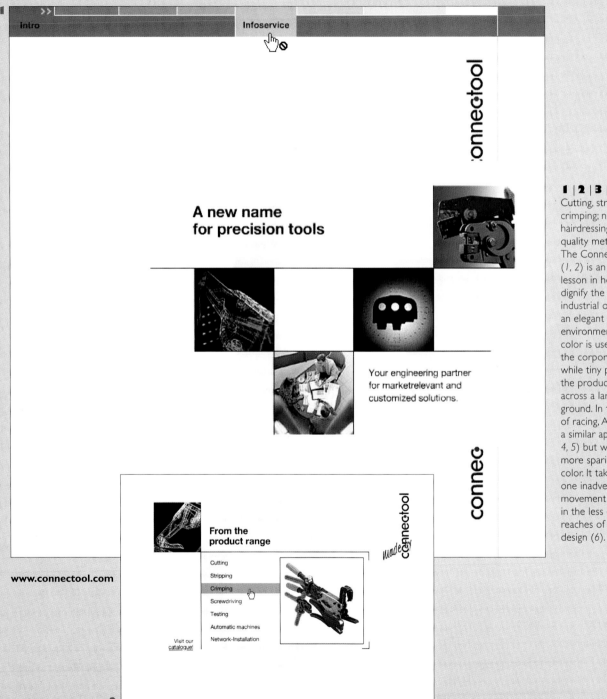

1 | 2 | 3 | 4 | 5 | 6
Cutting, stripping, and crimping; not hairdressing but high-quality metal-bashing. The Connectool site (*1, 2*) is an object lesson in how to dignify the prosaic industrial object in an elegant design environment. Spot color is used only in the corporate logo, while tiny pictures of the product float across a large white ground. In the world of racing, Acer adopts a similar approach (*3, 4, 5*) but with an even more sparing use of color. It takes only one inadvertent finger movement to land up in the less discreet reaches of page design (*6*).

3

Products About Contact Store

ACER**RACING**

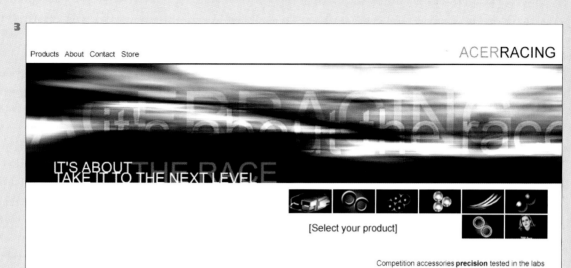

IT'S ABOUT
TAKE IT TO THE NEXT LEVEL

[Select your product]

Competition accessories **precision** tested in the labs
and proven on the track. You can feel the difference
with ACER Racing. Take it to the next level.

This site realized by EN|VISION
interactive

› Products About Contact Store | Home

ACER**RACING**

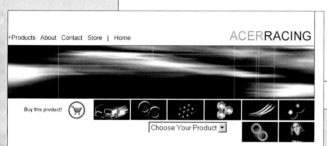

Buy this product!

Choose Your Product ▼

Statistics and information

ULTRA O PERFORMANCE SERIES
SUSPENSION O RINGS

The only professional suspension o-ring to
combine the lowest coefficient of friction, internal
lubrication, and the highest tear resistance. The
longest lasting, smoothest o-ring **ever** for the
smoothest suspension movement. What can
these o-rings do for you?

› Extend rebuild intervals

5

Products About Contact Store | Home

ACER**RACING**

Buy this product!

Choose Your Product ▼

What could be cooler than your own
ACER Racing T-Shirt?

Get an Acer Racing T-Shirt
for only $15. Make sure to
specify your size. Available in
L and XL.

www.acerracing.com

6

www.aceracing.com

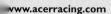

168

1 | 2
Cultural confusion in
Milwaukee. Beer is
now music. And the
light blond hues of
the product are
nowhere to be seen.
Java and Flash drive a
frantic dark palette
of opposing red and
blue against the
customary techno
graph paper.

www.mgdtaproom.com

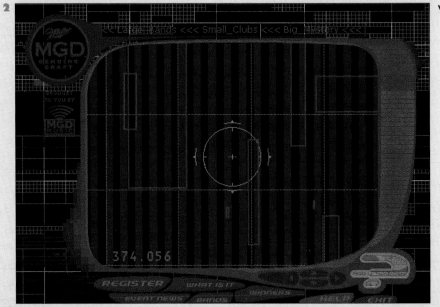

www.binding.de

www.grolsch.nl

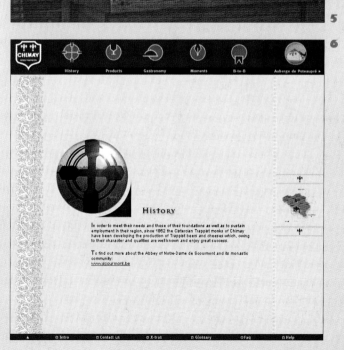

5

6

www.fullers.co.uk

|4|5|6

our European
breweries tackle the
art of promotion in
more conventional
style.

www.chimay.com

1 | 2

Welcome, in German and Italian. Druckindustrie Nord printers (1) plant an elegant foot in the digital doorway. Gone is the usual printer's identity of oversize CMYK dots and fluttering sheets of paper—there remains only a faint shadow of meshing cogs in the background. Giglio (2) adopts the same gray and orange uniform for its Sicilian fashion store.

www.vdnord.de

www.giglio.com

ww.fujifilm.com

www.josecuervo.com

4

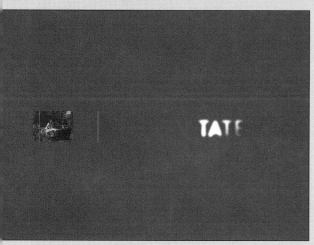

6

"We are the same human being all sharing the same planet." His Holiness the Dalai Lama

| 2 | 3 | 4

www.tate.org.uk.

www.goa.org.uk

eb-page design is
erely a branch of
oking; whatever the
redients, the plate
st appear appetiz-
. These four
amples of the
romatic present are
inters to the
mediate future. Fuji
offers cool inter-
ive cartography
er a salad bed of
their house packaging
color. The UK's Tate
Modern gallery site
(5), opens up with a
soft jelly logo drizzled
over raspberry sauce.
Cuervo tequila (4)
clings joyfully to
heritage design on a
bed of modern
Mexicana, while Goa
(6) offers a musical
smorgasbord.

HTML COLOR MECHANICS

The tiny rosette of dots that is the basis of the four-color print process makes a dull bouquet alongside the monitor's glowing phosphors. Although the printed page has a fundamental resolution about four times finer than the screen, its apparent superiority is more than negated by the screen's much greater contrast range and highly saturated color values. The typical user, moreover, sits at least twice as far away from the screen as from a book, adding more apparent sharpness to the screen image.

With sufficient processing power, current monitors can deliver over 16 million different colors. This is as near "true" color as makes no practical difference. Prehistoric monitors could only turn pixels on and off—screens were black-and-white (or, variously, black and green, or orange). This was "one-bit" color depth, and great was the joy in the land when the frontiers were gradually pushed back through four-bit, giving 16 (2^4) colors, and then the eight-bit 256 (2^8) games standard, right up to 24-bit (2^{24}) with 16,777,216 colors.

Large numbers of this order won't work reliably on the Web. A handy compromise for now is a 256-color range. Subtract the 40 colors demanded for its own purposes by the computer's operating system, and you are left with 216. This offers an elegant cube with six units per edge. Another sum: 6 x 6 x 6 = 216. A cube has eight convenient corners—and the red, green, and blue electron guns at the back of the screen, when either full on or off, can produce eight combinations of color.

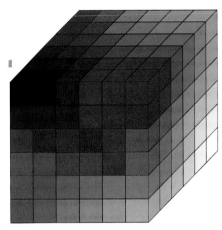

1
The 216-color cube shows seven of its eight corners (*left*). Yellow (red and green mixed at full strength) is hidden at the back left corner.

Put these extremes at the corners of the cube and string the intermediate colors along each edge to give a 20 percent difference between each color. In other words, the guns have a six-step range between 0 (completely off) and 255 (full on).

2

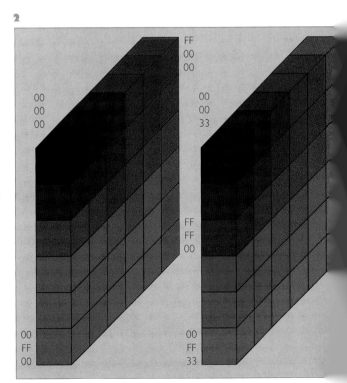

2
Filleted out, the cube reveals all 216 colors. Black (no signal at all) and white (all three guns full on) are found at diagonally opposite corners.

Only one hurdle remains. The computer needs a single character to represent numeric values. Hexadecimal comes to the rescue. In hexadecimal there are 16 values, represented by the numerals 0–9 followed by the characters A–F. Only six of these values concern us here, because of the 20 percent gap between one value and the next. In HTML code, colors are represented by settings for the red/green/blue guns in the paired form rrggbb. Since it's difficult to visualize a color labeled CC0033, Web-design software conceals the mathematics and calls it "pinkish red." Such programs will accept intermediate colors (like B0C4DE, "light steel blue"), but they will appear dithered on 256-color screens.

The flattened cube is shown (within the limitations of the four-color process) on the following two pages. The two subsequent pages then show patches of 18 selected colors overlaid with 12 different shades.

3

Value	%	Hex
0 =	0% =	00
51 =	20% =	33
102 =	40% =	66
153 =	60% =	99
204 =	80% =	CC
255 =	100% =	FF

4

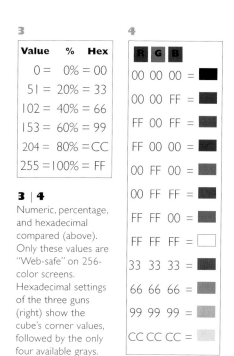

R	G	B	
00	00	00	=
00	00	FF	=
FF	00	FF	=
FF	00	00	=
00	FF	00	=
00	FF	FF	=
FF	FF	00	=
FF	FF	FF	=
33	33	33	=
66	66	66	=
99	99	99	=
CC	CC	CC	=

3 | 4
Numeric, percentage, and hexadecimal compared (above). Only these values are "Web-safe" on 256-color screens. Hexadecimal settings of the three guns (right) show the cube's corner values, followed by the only four available grays.

175

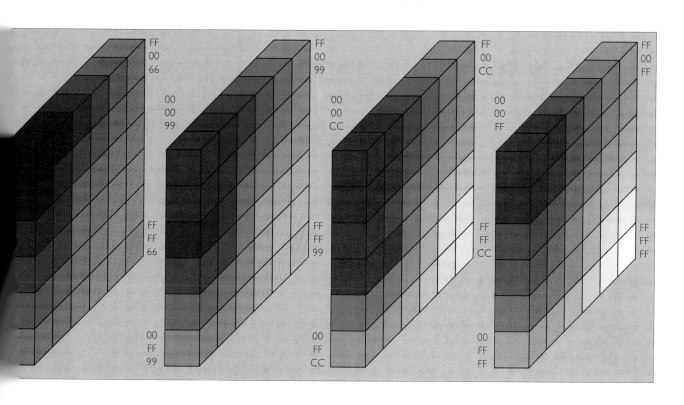

330000	333300	336600	339900	33CC00	33FF00	66FF00	66CC00	669900
330033	333333	336633	339933	33CC33	33FF33	66FF33	66CC33	669933
330066	333366	336666	339966	33CC66	33FF66	66FF66	66CC66	669966
330099	333399	336699	339999	33CC99	33FF99	66FF99	66CC99	669999
3300CC	3333CC	3366CC	3399CC	33CCCC	33FFCC	66FFCC	66CCCC	6699CC
3300FF	3333FF	3366FF	3399FF	33CCFF	33FFFF	66FFFF	66CCFF	6699FF
0000FF	0033FF	0066FF	0099FF	00CCFF	00FFFF	99FFFF	99CCFF	9999FF
0000CC	0033CC	0066CC	0099CC	00CCCC	00FFCC	99FFCC	99CCCC	9999CC
000099	003399	006699	009999	00CC99	00FF99	99FF99	99CC99	999999
000066	003366	006666	009966	00CC66	00FF66	99FF66	99CC66	999966
000033	003333	006633	009933	00CC33	00FF33	99FF33	99CC33	999933
000000	003300	006600	009900	00CC00	00FF00	99FF00	99CC00	999900

666600	663300	660000	FF0000	FF3300	FF6600	FF9900	FFCC00	FFFF00
666633	663333	660033	FF0033	FF3333	FF6633	FF9933	FFCC33	FFFF33
666666	663366	660066	FF0066	FF3366	FF6666	FF9966	FFCC66	FFFF66
666699	663399	660099	FF0099	FF3399	FF6699	FF9999	FFCC99	FFFF99
6666CC	6633CC	6600CC	FF00CC	FF33CC	FF66CC	FF99CC	FFCCCC	FFFFCC
6666FF	6633FF	6600FF	FF00FF	FF33FF	FF66FF	FF99FF	FFCCFF	FFFFFF
9966FF	9933FF	9900FF	CC00FF	CC33FF	CC66FF	CC99FF	CCCCFF	CCFFFF
9966CC	9933CC	9900CC	CC00CC	CC33CC	CC66CC	CC99CC	CCCCCC	CCFFCC
996699	993399	990099	CC0099	CC3399	CC6699	CC9999	CCCC99	CCFF99
996666	993366	990066	CC0066	CC3366	CC6666	CC9966	CCCC66	CCFF66
996633	993333	990033	CC0033	CC3333	CC6633	CC9933	CCCC33	CCFF33
996600	993300	990000	CC0000	CC3300	CC6600	CC9900	CCCC00	CCFF00

177

	000000	666666	CCCCCC	FF0000	00FF00	0000FF	FFFF00	FF00FF	00FFFF
000066									
330000									
999966									
FF99FF									
006600									
FF6600									
990000									
FF6666									
333366									
663300									
330099									
FFCC33									

178

| CC0000 | CC00CC | 0000CC | 00CCCC | 00CC00 | CCCC00 | 336633 | 99CC99 | CCFF66 |

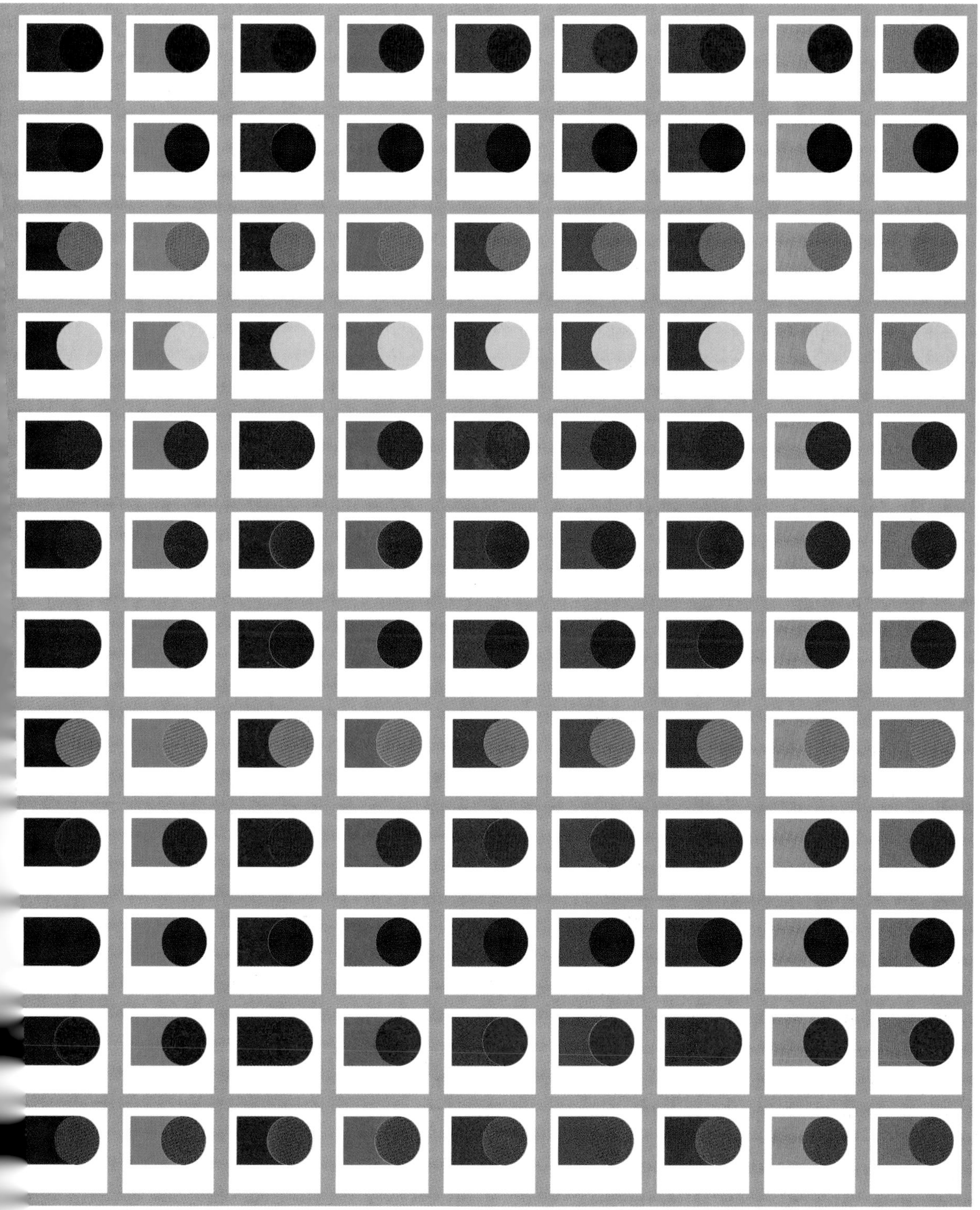

000066

330000

999966

FF99FF

179

006600

FF6600

990000

FF6666

333366

663300

330099

FFCC33

GLOSSARY

4-bit The allocation of four bits of memory to each pixel, giving an image or screen display of 16 grays or colors (a row of four bits can be written in 16 different combinations: 0000, 0001, 1001, 0110, etc.).

8-bit Of display monitors or digital images—the allocation of eight data bits to each pixel, producing a display or image of 256 grays or colors (a row of eight bits can be written in 256 different combinations: 0000000, 00000001, 10000001, 00111100, and so on).

16-bit color A facility in some image-editing applications, such as Photoshop, that allows you to work on images in 16-bit-per-channel mode rather than 8-bit mode—RGB images use three 8-bit channels (totaling 24 bits), whereas CMYK images use four 8-bit channels (totaling 32 bits). A 16-bit-per-channel image provides finer control over color, but because an RGB image totals 48 bits (16 × 3) and a CMYK image totals 64 bits (16 × 4), the resulting file size is considerably larger than an 8-bit-per-channel image.

24-bit color The allocation of 24 bits of memory to each pixel, giving a possible screen display of 16.7 million colors (a row of 24 bits can be written in 16.7 million different combinations of 0s and 1s). Twenty-four bits are required for CMYK separations—eight bits for each.

absolute colorimetry Calibrating the color performance of a device relative to an "absolute" CIE white (e.g. D50), rather than to the device's natural white point.

achromatic A color that has no saturation, or "chroma," such as black or white.

additive colors The color model describing the primary colors of transmitted light: red, green, and blue (RGB). Additive colors can be mixed to form all other colors in photographic reproduction and computer display monitors.

adjustment profile An adjustment that alters image appearance, applied during the creation of a link.

alpha channel A place where information regarding the transparency of a pixel is kept. In image files this is a separate channel—additional to the three RGB or four CMYK channels—where "masks" are stored, simulating the physical material used in platemaking to shield parts of the plate from light.

anti-aliasing A technique of optically eliminating the jagged effect of bitmapped images or text reproduced on low-resolution devices such as monitors. This is achieved by blending the color at the edges of the object with its background by averaging the density of the range of pixels involved. Anti-aliasing is also sometimes employed to filter texture maps, such as those used in 3-D applications, to prevent moiré patterns.

ASCII *(pronounced "asskee")* Acronym for the American Standard Code for Information Interchange, a code that assigns a number to the 256 letters, numbers, and symbols (including carriage returns and tabs) that can be typed on a keyboard. ASCII is the cross-platform, computer-industry standard, text-only file format.

attribute (1) The specification applied to a character, box, or other item. Character attributes include font, size, style, color, shade, scaling, kerning, etc.

attribute (2) A characteristic of an HTML tag that is identified alongside the tag in order to describe it.

background The area of an image upon which the principal subject, or foreground, sits.

background color/tint In graphics applications, a color or tint that has been applied to the background of any item, such as a page, text box, or illustration.

banding An aberration that occurs in the electronic reproduction of graduated tints, when the ratio of halftone screen ruling and output resolution is incorrect, causing a "stepped" appearance. The maximum number of achievable levels of tone is 256 (the PostScript limit) for each of the four process colors (CMYK); so to calculate the optimum imagesetter resolution, multiply the halftone screen ruling by 16 (the square root of 256—each imagesetter dot is constructed on a matrix of 16 × 16 pixels). Therefore, to minimize the chance of banding in a single color image to be printed with a halftone screen ruling of 150 lpi, the maximum levels of gray can be achieved if it is output by the imagesetter at 2400 dpi (150 × 16). Banding can also occur when the percentage values of a large area of a graduated single color tint are very close (40–50%, for example).

binary system An arithmetical system that uses 2 as its base, meaning that it can only be represented by two possible values—1 or 0, on or off, something or nothing, negative or positive, small or large, etc.

binary code The computer code, based on 1 or 0, that is used to represent a character or instruction. For example, the binary code 01100010 represents a lower case "b."

binary file A file in which data is described in binary code rather than text. Binary files typically hold pictures, sounds, or a complete application program.

bit A commonly used acronym for binary digit, the smallest piece of information a computer can use. Each alphabet character requires eight bits (called a **byte**) to store it.

bit density The number of bits occupying a particular area or length—per inch of magnetic tape, for example.

bit depth The number of bits assigned to each pixel on a monitor, scanner, or image file. One-bit, for example, will only produce black and white (the bit is either on or off), whereas 8-bit will generate 256 grays or colors (256 is the maximum number of permutations of a string of eight 1s and 0s), and 24-bit will produce 16.7 million colors (256 × 256 × 256). Also called **color depth**.

bitmap Strictly speaking, any text character or image composed of dots. A bitmap is a "map" describing the location and binary state (on or off) of "bits"; it defines the complete collection of pixels or dots that comprise an image (on a monitor, for example).

bitmapped font A font in which the characters are made up of dots, or pixels, as distinct from an outline font, which is drawn from vectors. Bitmapped fonts generally accompany PostScript "Type 1" fonts and are used to render the fonts' shape on screen (they are sometimes called screen fonts). To draw the shape accurately on screen, your computer must have a bitmap installed for each size (they are also called fixed-size fonts), although this is not necessary if you have ATM installed, as this uses the outline, or printer version, of the font. TrueType fonts are "outline" and so do not require a bitmapped version.

bitmapped graphic An image made up of dots or pixels, and usually generated by paint or image-editing applications, as distinct from the vector images of object-oriented drawing applications.

black generation The process of creating the black channel, and its effects on the color channels when converting RGB to CMYK.

blend(ing) The merging of two or more colors, forming a gradual transition from one to the other. Most graphics applications offer the facility for creating blends from any mix and any percentage of process colors. The quality of the blend is limited by the number of shades of a single color that can be reproduced without visible "banding." Since this limit is determined by the PostScript maximum of 256 levels, banding may become more visible when the values of a single color are very close (30–60%, for example). However, blending two or more colors reduces the risk of banding.

brightness The amount of light reflected by a color.

brightness range The range of tones in a photographic subject, from the darkest to the lightest.

bump map A bitmap image file, normally grayscale, most frequently used in 3-D applications for modifying surfaces or applying textures. The gray values in the image are assigned height values, with black representing the troughs and white the peaks. Bump maps are used in the form of digital elevation models (DEMs) for generating cartographic relief maps.

byte A single group made up of eight bits (0s and 1s) that is processed as one unit. It is possible to configure eight 0s and 1s in only 256 different permutations; thus a byte can represent any value between 0 and 255—the maximum number of ASCII characters, one byte being required for each.

CAD (computer-aided design) Any design carried out using a computer. However, the term is generally used with reference to 3-D design, such as product design or architecture, where a computer software application is used to construct and develop complex structures.

CAD/CAM (computer-aided design and manufacture) Any manufacturing process in which computers are used to assist and control the entire operation from initial concept to finished product.

calibration The process of adjusting a machine or item of hardware to conform to a known scale or standard so that it performs more accurately. In graphic reproduction it is important that the various devices and materials used in the production chain, such as scanners, monitors, imagesetters, and printing presses, conform to a consistent set of measures in order to achieve true fidelity, particularly where color is concerned. Calibration of reproduction and display devices is generally carried out with a **densitometer**.

characterization Measuring the color characteristics of a device and comparing the measurements to standard reference values. In color management, the measure of these deviations results in a device profile.

chroma The intensity, or purity, of a color; thus, its degree of saturation.

chromaticity The hue and saturation of a color sample.

Cibachrome A proprietary process for obtaining photographic color prints directly from transparencies, developed by Agfa.

CIE (Commission Internationale de l'Eclairage) International organization which defined a visual color model that forms the basis for colorimetric measurements of color.

CIE L*a*b* color space A three-dimensional color model based on the system devised by CIE for measuring color. L*a*b* color is designed to maintain consistent color regardless of the kind of device used to create or output the image, whether a scanner, monitor or printer. L*a*b* color consists of a luminance or lightness component (L) and two chromatic components: green to red (a) and

blue to yellow (b). Without the asterisks, it is the internal color model used by Adobe Photoshop when converting from one color mode to another; and "Lab mode" is useful for working with Kodak PhotoCD images. CIE L*a*b* values are mathematically convenient but non-intuitive to most people, hence L*a*b* color editing tools are uncommon.

CIE XYZ A CIE color space defined in three dimensions (XYZ). These coordinates represent the amount of red, green, and blue light necessary to match a specific color.

CLUT Acronym for Color Look-Up Table. A preset table of colors (to a maximum of 256) that the operating system uses when in 8-bit mode. CLUTs are also attached to individual images saved in 8-bit "indexed" mode—that is, when an application converts a 24-bit image (one with millions of colors) to 8-bit, it draws up a table ("index") of up to 256 of the most frequently used colors in the image (the total number of colors depending on where the image will be viewed—Mac, Windows, or Web, for example). If a color in the original image does not appear in the table, the application either chooses the closest one or simulates it by "dithering" colors that are available in the table.

CMY (cyan, magenta, yellow) The primary colors of the "subtractive" color model, created when you subtract red, green, or blue from white light. In other words, if an object reflects green and blue light but absorbs (subtracts) red, then it will appear to you as cyan. Cyan, magenta, and yellow are the basic printing-process colors.

CMYK (cyan, magenta, yellow, and black) The four printing-process colors based on the subtractive color model (black is represented by the letter K, which stands for key plate). In color reproduction most of the colors are achieved by cyan, magenta, and yellow, the theory being that when all three are combined, they produce black. However, this is rarely achievable—and would be undesirable as too much ink would be used, causing problems with drying time, etc. For this reason, black is used to add density to darker areas—while, to compensate, smaller amounts of the other colors are used (this also has cost benefits, as black is cheaper than colored inks). The degree of color that is "removed" is calculated by a technique known as undercolor removal (UCR).

Color-Key™ A proprietary dry-proofing system developed by 3M.

ColorSync Apple Computer's implementation of the ICC standard.

color The visual interpretation of the various wavelengths of reflected or refracted light.

color bar The color device printed on the edge of color proofs or in the trim area of press sheets which enables the repro house and printer to check—by eye or with instruments—the fidelity of color separations and the accuracy of printing. The color bar helps to monitor such things as ink density, paper stability, dot gain, trapping, and so on. Also called a "codet."

color break The edge between two areas of color in an image.

color cast A bias in a color image that can be either intentional or undesirable. If the former, it is usually made at proof-correction stage to enhance the color of an image; if the latter, the cast could be due to any of a number of causes occurring when the image was photographed, scanned, manipulated on computer, output, proofed, or printed.

color chart A printed reference chart used in color reproduction to select or match color tints made from percentage variations of the four process colors. When using a color chart, for absolute accuracy you should have one prepared by your chosen printer and printed on the actual paper that will be used for the job—a situation that, in practice, is highly unlikely.

color correction The process of adjusting color values in reproduction in order to achieve the desired result. Although this can occur at scanning or image-manipulation stage, color correction is generally carried out after "wet" proofing (proofs created using process-color inks) or, as a very limited last resort, on press.

color engine A software utility that applies links to images to transform them from one mode to another.

color filters Thin sheets of transparent material, such as glass or gelatin, placed over a camera lens to modify the quality of light or colors in an image.

color gamut Gamut, or **color space**, describes the full range of colors achievable by any single device on the reproduction chain. While the visible spectrum contains many millions of colors, not all of them are achievable by all devices, and, even if the color gamuts for different devices overlap, they will never match exactly—for example, the 16.7 million colors that can be displayed on a monitor cannot be printed on a commercial four-color press. For this reason, various color-management systems (CMS) have been devised to maintain consistency of color gamuts across various devices.

colorimeter A device that is used for measuring tristimulus values (the quantities of RGB; see **tristimulus values**).

colorimetric Measured or expressed in terms of tristimulus values (quantities of RGB).

color library An application support file that contains predefined colors. These may be the application's default colors, or colors defined by you, or other predefined color palettes or tables.

color-management module (CMM) A profile for managing and matching colors accurately across different platforms and devices. CMMs conform to a color-management system (CMS), such as that defined by the International Color Consortium (ICC). CMMs interpret the ICC profiles that describe the RGB and CMYK color spaces on your computer. There are usually ICC profiles installed on your computer by ICC-compliant applications such as Adobe Photoshop; or you can create your own. The selected profile is then embedded in the image you are working on, so that it can later be used as a reference by other devices in the production process. You may find a variety of CMMs already on your computer: those built in to ICC-compliant applications (usually the best if you are unsure of how to use CMMs); the Kodak Digital Science Color Management System® (primarily for use with images using the Kodak PhotoCD format); or CMMs specified by the

computer's operating system, such as Apple ColorSync and Microsoft ICM.

color-management system (CMS) The name given to a method devised to provide accuracy and consistency of color representation across all devices in the color-reproduction chain—scanners, monitors, printers, imagesetters, and so on. Typical CMSs include the ones defined by the International Color Consortium (ICC), Kodak's Digital Science Color Management System, Apple's ColorSync, and Microsoft's ICM.

color model The method of defining or modifying color. Although there are many proprietary color models, such as PANTONE®, FOCOLTONE, TRUMATCH, TOYO, and DIC, the two generic models are those based on the way light is transmitted—the "additive" and "subtractive" color models. The additive color model is used, for example, in computer monitors, which transmit varying proportions of red, green, and blue (RGB) light which we interpret as different colors. By combining the varying intensities of RGB light, we can simulate the range of colors found in nature. When 100% values of all three are combined, we perceive white; and if there is no light, we see nothing or, rather, black. The subtractive color model is based on the absorption (i.e., subtraction) and reflection of light. Printing inks are an example of this—if you subtract 100% values of either red, green, or blue from white light, you create cyan, magenta, or yellow.

color picker (1) A color model displayed on a computer monitor. Color pickers may be specific to an application such as Adobe Photoshop, or to a third-party color model such as PANTONE®, or to the operating system running on your computer.

color picker (2) A book of printed color samples that are carefully defined and graded from which you can select spot colors. Color pickers generally conform to a color model such as PANTONE®, so you can be confident that the color you choose will be faithfully reproduced by the printer—unlike a "color chart," which is generally used to select colors made up from process-color inks.

color space See **color gamut**.

color swatch A sample of a specific color, taken either from a color chart or color picker, or from some other printed example, and used as a guide either for specification or reproduction of spot colors or process tints.

color table A predefined table, or "index," of colors used to determine a specific color model—for example, for converting an image to CMYK. A color table, or "CLUT," also describes the palette of colors used to display an image.

color temperature A measure, or composition, of light. This is defined as the temperature—measured in degrees Kelvin (a scale based on absolute darkness rising to incandescence)—to which a black object would need to be heated to produce a particular color of light. A tungsten lamp, for example, measures 2,900°K, whereas the temperature of direct sunlight is around 5,000°K and is considered the ideal viewing standard in the graphic arts.

color transparency (film) A photographic image on transparent film generated, after processing, as a positive image. Color transparencies are ideal as originals for color separations for process printing because they offer a greater range of colors than is provided by reflective prints. Color-transparency film is supplied for a variety of camera formats—typically 35mm, 2¼in square, and 4 x 5in. Color transparencies are also variously known as trannies, color trannies, slides (which generally refers to 35mm), chromes, and color-reversal film.

color value The tonal value of a color when related to a light-to-dark scale of pure grays.

color wheel Circular diagram representing the complete spectrum of visible colors.

commercial color The term (sometimes used derogatorily) applied to color images generated by desktop scanners, as opposed to high-resolution reproduction scanners.

complementary colors Two colors directly opposite each other on the color wheel that, when combined, form white or black, depending on the color model.

Component Video A QuickTime "codec" (compression setting) that generates a 2:1 compression. Being limited to 16-bit color depth, it is best suited to archiving movies.

composite color file The low-resolution file that combines the four CMYK files of an image saved in the five-file DCS (desktop color separation) format and which is used to preview the image and position it in layouts. Since the composite file is not the one used for separations, you should take care when using it with runaround text. If, for example, you define a path in QuarkXPress, that path will not be contained in the four separation files and the runaround will not work as you planned.

composite video A video "bus," or signal, in which all the color information is combined, such as in the "video out" port on older VCRs (video cassette recorders). This results in loss of quality. On computer monitors, quality is maintained by keeping each of the RGB color signals separate.

content provider A provider of information on the Web, as distinct from an Internet service provider (ISP).

continuous tone (ct) An image that contains infinite continuous shades between the lightest and darkest tones, as distinct from a line illustration, which has only one shade. Usually used to describe an image before it is either broken up by the dots of a halftone screen for printing or "dithered" into a pattern of colors for viewing on low-resolution monitors. Also called **contone**.

contrast The degree of difference between adjacent tones in an image (or computer monitor), from the lightest to the darkest. High contrast describes an image with light highlights and dark shadows but with few shades in between, whereas a low-contrast image is one with even tones and few dark areas or highlights.

convergence In color monitors, the adjustment of the three RGB beams so that they come together in the right place on the screen.

cool colors A subjective term used to describe colors that have a blue or green bias.

cosmetics Sometimes used to describe the overall appearance of an image, such as color, contrast, sharpness, etc.

CRD (Color Rendering Dictionary) A table that can be downloaded to a PostScript Level II RIP to control PostScript color handling.

cyan (c) With magenta and yellow, one of the three subtractive primaries and one of the three process colors used in four-color printing. Sometimes referred to as **process blue**.

cyan printer The plate or film used to print cyan ink in four-color process printing.

DCS (desktop color separation) A file format used for outputting image files to color separation. DCS files combine a low-resolution image for displaying onscreen with high-resolution EPS format data for color separations. There are two versions of DCS format files: namely, DCS 1.0 and DCS 2.0. DCS 1.0 files comprise five files—a single low-resolution composite file for placing in a layout, plus four high-resolution separation files, one each for cyan, magenta, yellow, and black. The DCS 2.0 format allows you to save spot colors with the image, which you can choose to save as a single file (thus saving space) or as multiple files, as in DCS 1.0. Clipping paths can also be saved with both DCS 1.0 and DCS 2.0.

DDCP (direct digital color proof) Any color proof made directly from digital data without using separation films, such as those produced on an ink-jet printer.

definition The overall quality—or clarity—of an image, determined by the combined subjective effect of graininess (or resolution in a digital image) and sharpness.

degauss(ing) The technique of removing, or neutralizing, any magnetic field that may have built up over time in a color monitor. Magnetism can distort the fidelity of color display. Since most modern monitors perform a degauss automatically, this process is usually only necessary on older monitors.

degradability The term applied to Web browsers able to support new advances in HTML technologies while at the same time serving browsers based on previous versions of the technologies.

Delta E (dE) A measurement of color error or difference based on L*a*b* coordinates.

dense An image that is too dark.

densitometer A precision instrument used to measure the optical density and other properties of color and light in positive or negative transparencies, printing film, reflection copy, or computer monitors. Also called a **color coder**. *See* **calibration**.

density The darkness of tone or color in any image. In a transparency this refers to the amount of light that can pass through it, thus determining the darkness of shadows and the saturation of color. A printed highlight can not be any lighter in color than the color of the paper it is printed on, while the shadows can not be any darker than the quality and volume of ink that the printing process will allow.

density range The maximum range of tones in an image, measured as the difference between the maximum and minimum densities (the darkest and lightest tones).

desaturate To reduce the strength or purity of color in an image, thus making it grayer.

desaturated color Color containing a large amount of gray in proportion to the hue.

descreen(ing) The technique of removing a halftone dot pattern from an image to avoid an undesirable moiré pattern occurring when a new halftone screen is applied. This can be achieved in image-editing applications by using built-in filters (effects) to blur the image slightly and then sharpen it. However, you can achieve better results with dedicated image-enhancement applications that do this automatically using sophisticated interpolation methods—you can, for example, choose the amount of descreening according to the quality of printing or the fineness of the halftone, which can cover anything from fine art books to newspapers. *See* **interpolation**.

desktop color Color images prepared or generated using a desktop system, where an original is scanned by a desktop scanner, adjusted on a desktop computer, and positioned and output using a page-layout application. The term is often used—not necessarily derogatorily—to indicate color reproduction of an inferior quality to that produced on a high-end CEPS system.

device-dependent color Color space that is specific to a device. A scanner's RGB values are unrelated to a printer's CMYK values for the same color, because both values depend on the device where the image is generated or from which it is output.

device-independent color An intermediate color space to which scanners and printers are calibrated and through which images are translated regardless of what they are prepared or output on.

dichroic filter A filter that permits certain wavelengths of light to pass through, while preventing others.

dichroic fog An aberration in processed film, appearing as a red or green cloud, caused by an imbalance of chemicals in the developer.

diffraction The scattering of light waves as they strike the edge of an opaque surface. In the conventional preparation of halftones, this can affect dot formations.

digital dot A dot generated by a digital computer or device. Digital dots are all the same size whereas halftone dots vary, so, in digitally generated halftones several dots—up to 256 (on a 16 x 16 matrix)—are required to make up each halftone dot.

digital photography The process of either capturing an image with digital equipment or manipulating photographic images on a computer, or both. In both cases, the term describes photographs that are recorded or manipulated in binary form, rather than on film.

digital video interactive (DVI) A computer chip developed by Intel that compresses and decompresses video images.

digitize To convert anything—for example, text, images or sound—into binary form, so that it can be digitally processed, manipulated, stored, and reconstructed. In other words, transforming analog to digital.

digitizer Strictly speaking, any hardware device (such as a scanner or camera) that converts drawn or photographed images into binary code, so you can work with them on a computer. However, the term is more commonly used to refer specifically to "digitizing tablets".

dither(ing) A technique of interpolation that calculates the average value of adjacent pixels. This technique is used either to add extra pixels to an image—to smooth an edge, for example, as in anti-aliasing—or to reduce the number of colors or grays in an image by replacing them with average values that conform to a predetermined palette of colors. For example, when an image containing millions of colors is converted ("resampled") to a fixed palette ("index") of, say, 256 colors. A color monitor operating in 8-bit color mode (256 colors) will automatically create a dithered pattern of pixels. Dithering is also used by some printing devices to simulate colors or tones.

dot A term that can mean one of three things: **(1)** a halftone dot (the basic element of a halftone image), **(2)** a machine dot (the dots produced by a laser printer or imagesetter), or **(3)** a scan dot (strictly speaking, pixels, which comprise a scanned bitmapped image). The three types of dot are differentiated by being expressed in lpi (lines per inch) for a halftone dot, dpi (dots per inch) for a machine dot, and ppi (pixels per inch) for a scan dot—although the latter is sometimes expressed, erroneously, in dpi. Thus, because the term "dot" is used to describe both halftone and machine dots, scan dots should always be referred to as pixels.

dot/stripe pitch The distance between the dots or pixels (actually, holes or slits in a screen mesh) on your monitor. The closer the dots, the finer the image display—though dot pitch has nothing to do with the resolution of the image itself.

dots per inch (dpi) A unit of measurement used to represent the resolution of devices such as printers and imagesetters; and also (erroneously) of monitors and images, whose resolution should more properly be expressed in pixels per inch (ppi). The closer the dots or pixels (i.e., the more there are to an inch), the better the quality. Typical resolutions are 72ppi for a monitor, 300dpi for a LaserWriter, and 2450dpi (or more) for an imagesetter.

Dynamic HTML/DHTML (Dynamic Hypertext Markup Language) A development of basic HTML code that enables you to ac such features as basic animations and high-lighted buttons to Web pages without relying on browser plug-ins. DHTML is built into version 4.0 and later-generation Web browsers.

EPS (encapsulated PostScript) A standard graphics file format used primarily for storing object-orientated (or "vector") graphics files generated by "drawing applications" such as Adobe Illustrator and Macromedia FreeHand (a vector is a tiny database giving information about both the magnitude and direction of a line or shape). An EPS file usually has two parts: one containing the PostScript code that tells the printer how to print the image, the other an onscreen preview, which can be in PICT, TIFF, or JPEG formats. Although used mainly for storing vector-based graphics, the EPS format is also widely used for storing bit-mapped images, particularly those used for desktop color separation (DCS). Such EPS files are encoded either as ASCII—a text-based description of an image—or in binary, which uses numbers rather than text to store data. Bitmapped EPS files that are to be printed from a Windows-based system use ASCII encoding, whereas ones to be printed in the Mac OS are usually saved with binary encoding, although not all printing software supports binary EPS files.

eyedropper tool In some applications, a tool for gauging the color of adjacent pixels.

fill In graphics applications, the content, such as color, tone, or pattern, applied to the inside of a shape, including type characters.

filter (1) Strictly speaking, in computer software a filter can be any component that provides the basic building blocks for processing data. However, the term is more commonly used to describe particular functions within an application (such as importing and exporting data in different file formats) or, in image-editing and drawing applications, those used for applying special effects to images.

filter (2) The colored-glass, tinted-gelatin, or cellulose-acetate sheets used in conventional color separation that absorb specific wavelengths of light, so the red, green, and blue components of an original can be separated to provide the cyan, magenta, yellow, and black films used in process printing.

final rendering The final computer generation of an image, once you have finally finished tweaking and agonizing (in low resolution). For example, application of the final surface texture, lighting, and effects to a 3-D object, scene, or animation. High-quality render-ings—particularly of animated scenes—require considerable processing power, so banks of linked computers are sometimes used to speed up the process, using a technique called **distributed rendering**.

flat Said of any image—original or printed—that lacks sufficient color or contrast.

flat-tint halftone A halftone image printed over a flat tint of color.

FM screening (frequency modulated screening) A method of screening an image for reproduction that uses a random pattern of dots to reproduce a continuous-tone image. Also known as **stochastic screening**.

FOCOLTONE A color-matching system in which all of the colors can be created by printing the specified process-color percentages.

four-color process Any printing process used to reproduce full-color images that have been separated into the three basic "process" colors (cyan, magenta, and yellow), with the fourth color (black) added for extra density.

full color Synonymous with four-color reproduction, the term most commonly used to describe process-color reproduction, but also used to describe multi-color fine art printing.

gamma A measure of contrast in a digital image, or in a photographic film or paper, or processing technique.

gamma correction Modification of the mid-tones of an image by compressing or expanding the range, thus altering the contrast. Also known as **tone correction**.

gamut compression Gamut mapping where the range of color values produced by an input device is compressed to fit into the smaller available gamut of the output device. Gamut compression can be crucial to good color reproduction, but colors that have been gamut compressed will seldom match the original.

gamut mapping The redistribution of color values from a color scanner to fit an output device. If the input gamut is larger than the output gamut, gamut mapping is the same as gamut compression. If the input gamut is smaller than the output gamut, the colors and contrast can be intensified through gamut expansion, or colors can be mapped to their exact equivalents (e.g., for digital proofing).

GCR (gray-component replacement) A color-separation technique in which black ink is used (instead of overlapping combinations of cyan, magenta, and yellow) to create gray shades. This technique avoids color variations and trapping problems during printing.

GIF (graphic interchange format) A bitmapped graphics format originally devised by Compuserve, an Internet service provider (now part of AOL), and sometimes (although rarely) referred to as Compuserve GIF. There are two specifications: GIF87a and, more recently, GIF89a, the latter providing additional features such as transparent backgrounds. The GIF format uses a lossless compression technique and thus does not squeeze files as much as the JPEG format, which is lossy (some data is discarded). For use in Web browsers, JPEG is the format of choice for tone images such as photographs, whereas GIF is more suitable for line images and other graphics such as text.

Gouraud shading A method, used in 3-D applications, of rendering by manipulating colors and shades selectively along the lines of certain vertices, which are then averaged across each polygon face in order to create a realistic light-and-shade effect.

gradation control A means of adjusting the contrast of specific tonal regions—either equally for all colorants or imaging channels, or separately for independent channels.

graduation/gradation/gradient The smooth transition from one color/tone to another. The relationship of reproduced lightness values to original lightness values in an imaging process, usually expressed as a **tone curve**.

gray Any neutral tone in the range between black and white, with no added color.

grayscale (1) A tonal scale printed in steps

185

from white to black, used for controlling the quality of both color and black-and-white photographic processing and also for assessing quality in halftone prints. A grayscale (also called a **step wedge**, **halftone step scale**, or **step tablet**) is sometimes printed on the edge of a sheet.

grayscale (2) The rendering of an image in a range of grays from white to black. In a digital image and on a monitor this usually means that an image is rendered with eight bits assigned to each pixel, giving a maximum of 256 levels of gray. Monochrome monitors (used increasingly rarely nowadays) can only display black pixels—in which case, grays are achieved by varying the number and positioning of black pixels using the technique called dithering.

green One of the three additive colors (red, green, and blue). See **additive colors**.

heraldic colors A standard system of representing the basic colors of heraldry by means of monochrome shading, hatching, etc. Used when color printing is impractical or unwarranted.

high-density In relation to all things digital, a term that invariably means "more"—and therefore "better."

hi-fi color Any process that increases the color range of an output imaging device (printer). Refers to extra inks and plates added to the standard CMYK set to improve the color gamut of offset lithography. The three main hi-fi systems are the Kuppers approach (CMYK + RGB), Pantone®Hexachrome™ (CMYK + orange and green), and MaxCMY (CMYK + extra CMY).

HSL (hue, saturation, lightness) A color model based upon the light transmitted either in an image or in your monitor—hue being the spectral color (the actual pigment color), saturation being the intensity of the color pigment (without black or white added), and brightness representing the strength of luminance from light to dark (the amount of black or white present). Variously called **HLS** (hue, lightness, saturation), **HSV** (hue, saturation, value), and **HSB** (hue, saturation, brightness).

HTML (Hypertext Markup Language) A text-based page-description language (PDL) used to format documents published on the World Wide Web, and which can be viewed with a Web browser.

http (Hypertext Transfer Protocol) A text-based set of rules by which files on the World Wide Web are transferred, defining the commands that Web browsers use to communicate with Web servers. The vast majority of World Wide Web addresses (URLs) are prefixed with http://.

hue Pure spectral color, which distinguishes a color from others. Red is a different hue from blue; and although light red and dark red may contain varying amounts of white or black, they may be the same hue.

ICC (International Color Consortium) Organization responsible for defining cross-application color standards.

indeterminate color A trapping term that describes an area of color comprising many colors, like a picture.

indexed color An image mode of a maximum of 256 colors used in some applications, such as Adobe Photoshop, to reduce the file size of RGB images so they can be used, for example, in multimedia presentations or Web pages. This is achieved by using an indexed table of colors ("a color look-up table," or CLUT) to which the colors in an image are matched. If a color in the image does not appear in the table (which can be either an existing table using a known palette of "safe" colors or one constructed from an image), then the application selects the nearest color or simulates it by arranging the available colors in a pattern (known as dithering).

interlacing A technique of displaying an image on a Web page in which the image reveals increasing detail as it downloads. Interlacing is usually offered as an option in image-editing applications when saving images in GIF, PNG, and progressive JPEG formats.

interpolation A computer calculation used to estimate unknown values that fall between known ones. One use of this process is to redefine pixels in bitmapped images after they have been modified in some way—for instance, when an image is resized (called "resampling") or rotated, or if color corrections have been made. In such cases the program makes estimates from the known values of other pixels lying in the same or similar ranges. Interpolation is also used by some scanning and image-manipulation software to enhance the resolution of images that have been scanned at low resolution. Inserting animation values between two keyframes of a movie sequence are also interpolations. Some applications allow you to choose an interpolation method—Photoshop, for example, offers Nearest Neighbor (for fast but imprecise results, which may produce jagged effects), Bilinear (for medium-quality results), and Bicubic (for smooth and precise results, but with slower performance).

inverting A feature of many applications whereby an image bitmap is reversed—so that, for example, the black pixels appear white and vice versa, making a negative image. Inverting also affects colors, turning blue to yellow, green to magenta, and red to cyan. The term "invert" is sometimes used synonymously (and confusingly) with "inverse," although the latter is more commonly used to mean reversing a selected area so that it becomes deselected, while the deselected area becomes selected.

IT8.7/1 An ISO-standard transmission color target. CIE data provided with each copy of the target enable scanning devices to be calibrated, characterized, or profiled in CIE terms.

IT8.7/2 An independent reflective version of the IT8.7/1, i.e., it has its own CIE data.

JPEG/JPG (Joint Photographic Experts Group) An ISO group that defines compression standards for bitmapped color images. The abbreviated form (pronounced "jay peg") gives its name to a lossy compressed file format in which the degree of compression from high compression/low quality to low compression/high quality can be defined by the user. This makes the format doubly suitable for images that are to be used either for print reproduction or for transmitting across networks such as the Internet—for viewing in Web browsers, for example. See **lossy compression**.

K, k (key plate) The black printing plate in four-color process printing, though the name is now more commonly used as shorthand for **process black**. Using the letter K rather than the initial B avoids confusion with blue, even though the abbreviation for process blue is C (cyan). See **CMYK**

Kelvin scale Temperature scale in which 0° is absolute zero. The "color temperature" of an object is the temperature a perfectly black radiating object would be if it glowed that shade of color. Average daylight, for example, is reckoned at 6,500°K for Europe and 5,000°K for North America. Blue colors mean higher temperatures, while reds mean lower temperatures.

knockout An area of background color that has been masked ("knocked out") by a foreground object, and so does not print. The opposite of "overprint."

lap To overlap colors in order to avoid registration problems ("trapping").

layer In some applications and Web pages, a level to which you can consign an element of the design you are working on. Selected layers may be active (meaning you can work on them) or inactive. Some applications may not provide a layering feature but nonetheless may lay items one on top of another in the order that you created them—and in some cases will allow you to send items to the back or bring them to the front.

light table/box A table or box with a translucent glass top lit from below, giving a color-balanced light suitable for viewing color transparencies and for color-matching them to proofs.

lightfast/colorfast Term used to describe ink or other material whose color is not affected by exposure to artificial or natural light, atmosphere, or chemicals.

lightness The tonal measure of a color relative to a scale running from black to white. Also called "brightness" or "value."

linearization The process of calibrating and compensating a device's inability to see or reproduce a straight line of tones. It is used to ensure an imagesetter reproduces the same halftone values as the imaging software.

link Mathematical look-up table (LUT) that translates colors from an input device into matching colors on an output device. Changes can be customized in the link to alter or improve the image.

lossless compression Methods of file compression in which no data is lost (as opposed to lossy compression). Both LZW and GIF are lossless-compression formats.

lossy compression Methods of file compression in which some data may be irretrievably lost during compression (as opposed to lossless compression). JPEG is a lossy format.

LZW (Lempel-Ziv-Welch) A widely supported lossless-compression method for bit-mapped images. It gives a compression ratio of 2:1 or more, depending on the range of colors in an image (an image that has large areas of flat color will yield higher compression ratios).

magenta (m) With cyan and yellow, one of the three subtractive primaries, and one of the three process colors used in four-color printing. Sometimes called **process red**.

mapping In computer parlance, assigning attributes—such as colors—to an image.

matt/matte A flat, slightly dull surface.

mean noon sunlight An arbitrary color temperature to which most daylight color films are balanced, based on the average color temperature of direct sunlight at midday in Washington, D.C. (5,400°K).

median filter A filter in some image-editing applications that removes small details by replacing a pixel with an averaged value of its surrounding pixels, ignoring extreme values.

metameric A color that changes hue under different lighting conditions.

midtones/middletones The range of tonal values in an image anywhere between the darkest and lightest—usually referring to those approximately half-way.

mode change Transformation of an image from one mode to another.

model Any control specification used for comparing the behavior of complex systems—a color model, for example.

monitor Your computer screen, or the unit that houses it. Variously referred to as screens, displays, VDUs, and VDTs. Monitors display images in color, grayscale, or monochrome, and are available in a variety of sizes (which are measured diagonally), ranging from 9in (229mm) to 21in (534mm) or more. Although most monitors use cathode-ray tubes, some contain liquid-crystal displays (LCDs), particularly portables and laptops and, more recently, gas plasma (large matrices of tiny, gas-filled glass cells).

monochrome/monochromatic Term used to describe an image of varying tones reproduced in a single color.

monochrome monitor A computer monitor that displays pixels as either black or white—rather than in shades of gray, as on a gray-scale monitor.

monotone Reproduction in a single color, without tonal variation.

MPEG (Motion Picture Experts Group) A compression format for squeezing full-screen VHS-quality digital video files and animations, providing huge compression ratios—of up to 200:1.

Munsell notation Color-ordering system specifying the three qualities/attributes: hue, value, and chroma. Expressed as HVC.

noise function A random-pattern generator for rendering colors in 3-D scenes—thus improving photorealism.

output target Series of color samples of the range of output-device colorant combinations. An output profile is created by putting the resulting CIE values in a table together with the colorant combinations that produced them.

PAL (phase alternation by line) Color-television system prevalent in most of Western Europe (but not in France). It uses 625 lines and displays images at 25 frames per second.

PANTONE® The registered trademark of Pantone Inc.'s system of color standards and control and quality requirements, in which each color bears a description of its formulation (in percentages) for subsequent printing. The PANTONE MATCHING SYSTEM® is used

187

throughout the world—consequently, colors specified by any designer can be matched exactly by any printer.

pastel shades Shades of color that are generally both lighter and less saturated than their equivalent bright hue.

patch A single sample.

PPD (PostScript Printer Description) A file describing the features and capabilities of a PostScript printer.

PEL (picture element) The smallest unit of a computer display that can be assigned an individual color and intensity (usually a pixel).

Phong shading A superior but time-consuming method of rendering 3-D images that computes the shading of every pixel. Usually used for final 32-bit renderings.

PICS animation Macintosh animation format that uses PICT images to create a sequence.

PICT A standard file format for storing bit-mapped and object-oriented images on Macintosh computers. Originally, the PICT format only supported eight colors, but a newer version, PICT2, supports 32-bit color.

pigment Particles of ground color, dissolved in a suitable medium to form ink or paint.

pixel Acronym for *picture element*. The smallest component of a digitally generated image, such as a single dot of light on a computer monitor. In its simplest form, one pixel corresponds to a single bit: 0 = off (white) and 1 = on (black). In color and grayscale images or monitors, a single pixel may correspond to several bits: an 8-bit pixel, for example, can be displayed in any of 256 colors (the total number of different configurations that can be achieved by eight 0s and 1s).

pixel depth The number of shades that a single pixel can display, determined by the number of bits used to display the pixel. One bit equals a single color (black); four bits (any permutation of four 1s and 0s, such as 0011 or 1001) produces 16 shades; and so on, up to 32 bits (although actually only 24—the other eight being reserved for functions like masking), which produces 16.7 million colors.

plug-ins A third-party filter or subprogram that supplements a host application.

PNG (portable network graphics) A file format for images used on the Web that provides 10–30% lossless compression, and supports variable transparency through alpha channels, cross-platform control of image brightness, and interlacing.

posterize/posterization To divide, by photographic or digital means, a continuous-tone image into either a predefined or arbitrary number of flat tones. Also known as **tone separation**.

PostScript Page-description language. PostScript code tells an output device how to construct page elements.

primary colors Pure colors from which theoretically (though not in practice) all other colors can be mixed. In printing, they are the "subtractive" pigment primaries (cyan, magenta, and yellow). The primary colors of light, or "additive" primaries, are red, green, and blue.

profile The colorimetric description of an input or output device.

progressive JPEG A digital-image format used for displaying JPEG images on Web pages. The image is displayed in progressively increasing resolutions as the data is downloaded to the browser. Also called **proJPEG**.

purity The degree of saturation of a color.

red One of the three additive primary colors (red, green, and blue).

reference colors Colors that are familiar to most people and thus easy to remember, like sky blue, grass green, etc.

registration color In many graphics applications, a default color that, when applied to items such as crop marks, will print on every separation plate.

relative colorimetry Values are relative to the white point of the device or image, rather than absolute CIE values.

relative densitometry Densities calculated by subtraction from the white point of the image or device. Relative reflection densities are calculated relative to white paper density. Relative transmission densities are calculated relative to the clear film base.

RGB (red, green, blue) The primary colors of the "additive" color model—used in video technology (including computer monitors) and also for graphics (for the Web and multimedia, for example) that will not ultimately be printed by the four-color (CMYK) process method.

RIP (Raster Imaging Processor) A device that converts page-description data (e.g., PostScript) into a form for output to an imagesetter.

sampling/sample A measurement of data—such as a pixel—averaged across a small "snapshot" of that data in order to make modifications. For example, assessing the density of shadows in an image by taking a sample across a few pixels with an appropriate tool (usually an "eyedropper").

saturation The variation in color of the same tonal brightness from none (gray), through pastel shades (low saturation), to pure color with no gray (high saturation, or "fully saturated"). Also called "purity" or "chroma."

screen angle The angle at which halftone screens of images printing in two or more colors are positioned to minimize undesirable dot patterns (moiré) when printed. The angle at which screens should be positioned depends upon the number of colors being printed, but the normal angles for four-color process printing are: cyan 105°, magenta 75°, yellow 90°, black 45°.

screen capture A "snapshot" of part or all of a monitor display. Also called a "screen shot," "screen grab," or "screen dump."

screen frequency The number of line rulings per inch (lpi) on a halftone screen.

separation filters The filters used to separate colors so that they can be printed individually. They each transmit about one-third of the spectrum.

separation guide A printed guide containing set of standard colors (such as cyan, magenta, yellow, red, green, blue, and black) which, when photographed alongside a color-critical subject (a painting, for example), allow the separation to be matched against the color-control bar printed alongside the image.

sepia A brown color, and also a monochrom

print in which the normal shades of gray appear as shades of brown.

shading In 3-D applications, the resulting color of a surface due to light striking it at an angle.

shadow areas The areas of an image that are darkest or densest.

sharpening Enhancing the apparent sharpness of an image by increasing the contrast between adjacent pixels.

smoothing The refinement of bitmapped images and text by a technique called "anti-aliasing" (adding pixels of an "in-between" tone). Smoothing is also used in some drawing and 3-D applications, where it is applied to a path to smooth a line, or to "polygons" to tweak resolution in the final rendering.

spectrophotometer Device for measuring luminous energy at various frequencies throughout the spectrum. Spectral data can be displayed as CMY density, L*a*b*, or XYZ.

spectrum Series of colors that results when normal white light is dispersed into its component parts by refraction through a prism.

specular map In 3-D applications, a texture map—such as those created by noise filters—that is used instead of specular color to control highlights.

specular reflectance The reflection (as by a mirror) of light rays at an angle equal to the angle at which it strikes a surface (angle of incidence).

subtractive colors The color model describing the primary colors of reflected light: cyan, magenta, and yellow (CMY). Subtractive colors form the basis for printed process colors.

SuperVGA (SVGA) A video display standard that supports 256 colors or more in a variety of resolutions.

surface In 3-D applications, the matrix of control points and line end points underlying a mapped texture or color.

swatch A color sample.

SWOP (Specifications for Web Offset Publications) A system of standards developed for the printing industry to aid consistency in the use of color-separation films and color proofing.

taper Referring to graduated tones and colors, the progression of one tone or color to the next.

taper angle The direction in which graduated tones or colors merge into one another.

Targa A digital-image format for 24-bit image files, commonly used by computer systems in the MS-DOS environment that contain the Truevision video board.

tertiary color The resulting color when two secondary colors are mixed.

TIFF, TIF (tagged image file format) A standard and popular graphics file format—originally developed by Aldus (now merged with Adobe) and Microsoft—that is used for scanned high-resolution bitmapped images, and for color separations. The TIFF format can be used for black-and-white, grayscale, and color images that have been generated on different computer platforms.

tint The resulting shade when white is added to a solid color.

tint sheet A preprinted sheet of halftone tints, patterns, and other designs that are cut and pasted onto camera-ready artwork.

tonal value/tone value The relative densities of tones in an image.

transparent GIF A feature of the GIF89a file format that allows you to place a non-rectangular image on the background color of a Web page.

trichromatic Comprising three colors.

tristimulus values The amounts of red, green, and blue light of specific bandwidths and wavelengths needed for a certain color.

tritone A halftone image that is printed using three colors. Typically, a black-and-white image is enhanced by addition of two colors. For example, when added to black, process yellow and magenta will produce a sepia-colored image.

TRUMATCH colors A system of color matching used for specifying process colors.

unsharp masking (USM) A traditional film-compositing technique used to "sharpen" an image. This can also be achieved digitally—by means of image-editing applications that use filters to enhance the details in a scanned image by increasing the contrast of pixels (the exact amount depending on various criteria such as the "threshold" specified and the radius of the area around each pixel).

unwanted colors Three color patches on color reproduction guides that record the same as the white patch when separated. For example, the blue, cyan, and magenta patches on a yellow separation record the same as the white patch.

wanted colors Three color patches on color reproduction guides that record the same as the black patch when separated. For example, the yellow, red and green patches on a yellow separation record the same as the black patch.

warm colors Any color with a hue veering toward red or yellow—as opposed to cool colors, which veer toward blue or green.

white light The color of light resulting from red, blue, and green being combined in equal proportions.

yellow (y) With cyan and magenta, one of the three subtractive primaries, and one of the three process colors used in four-color printing. Sometimes called **process yellow**.

189